MISTERO
BUFFO

MISTERO BUFFO

THE COLLECTED PLAYS OF DARIO FO

VOLUME TWO

TRANSLATED BY **RON JENKINS**

BASED ON THE EDITING OF FRANCA RAME

THEATRE COMMUNICATIONS GROUP   NEW YORK   2006

Mistero Buffo is published by Theatre Communications Group, Inc., 520 Eighth Avenue, 24th Floor, New York, NY 10018-4156.

This edition is published by arrangement of Giulio Einaudi Editore, Via Umberto Biancamano 2, 10121 Torino, Italy.

A Scandal of Epic Proportions: *Mistero Buffo* is reprinted from *Artful Laughter: Dario Fo and Franca Rame*, Aperture Press, New York, 2001. Reprinted by permission.

This publication is made possible in part with public funds from the New York State Council on the Arts, a State Agency.

TCG books are exclusively distributed to the book trade by Consortium Book Sales and Distribution, 1045 Westgate Drive, St. Paul, MN 55114.

Library of Congress Cataloging-in-Publication Data
Fo, Dario.
[Plays, English]
Mistero buffo: the collected plays of Dario Fo, volume two / by Dario Fo ; translated by Ron Jenkins.—1st ed.
p. cm.
ISBN-13: 978-1-55936-271-9 — ISBN-10: 1-55936-271-5 USA (pbk. : alk. paper)
1. Fo, Dario—Translations into English. I. Jenkins, Ronald Scott. II. Title.
PQ4866.O2 A24 2000

Cover photo is by Massimo Menghini
Cover design, text design and composition are by Lisa Govan

First Edition, June 2006

CONTENTS

ACKNOWLEDGMENTS

My deepest thanks to Franca Rame and Dario Fo for their friendship and collaboration. Thanks also to Francesa Silvano for reviewing the translation. And endless gratitude to my wife, Franziska, for her angelic inspiration.

A SCANDAL OF EPIC
PROPORTIONS: *MISTERO BUFFO*

Translator's Introduction by Ron Jenkins

FRANCO ZEFFIRELLI: I have no difficulty in declaring that Fo
is one of the great phenomena of the Italian theatre and
that his performances are almost always brilliant. And
I am also aware that the scurrilous quality of his theatre
comes from its roots in our theatrical history, for
instance, Plautus and the commedia dell'arte . . . And
now we come to the point. In my opinion, this type of
scurrilous theatre should not be presented to mass television audiences who are not prepared for it. I regret that
this work of Fo's, *Mistero Buffo*, because of its large audience, is becoming a pretext for a political controversy
that will end up harming the work and its author, given
the ridiculous comparisons that have been made between
Mistero Buffo and *Jesus* [Zeffirelli's television series on
the life of Christ] . . . We cannot force the provocations of
Fo into the homes of people who have nothing to do with
these arguments . . . the idea of broadcasting *Jesus* on
channel one and *Mistero* on channel two [in April 1977]
was a questionable choice. People coming out of the religious reverie that, for better or worse, *Jesus* could have
put them into, find themselves immersed in a climate of
violent de-sanctification. I wanted above all to create a
mood of pacification, of love. My *Jesus* was intended to

enter the lives of people without disturbing them . . . It doesn't seem right to me to subject the Gospels to satire . . .

DARIO FO: I accuse Zeffirelli of having cut out of his program the greatest moment of the Gospel tradition, not to mention the most popular, which is the episode of the wedding at Cana. Zeffirelli has censored the moment of joy, the great festival of a community, which is rooted in a very important fact: the union, also sexual, of two young people. This "cut" is in opposition to the popular tradition of reading the Gospels as the return of springtime. The great ritual of resurrection is already there in that episode, in the transformation of water into wine, in the almost Dionysian pleasure of love. To remove this aspect is to follow the catechism and to support the vision of the ecclesiastic powers of the church, and to ignore above all the more culturally elevated point of view found in the great popular tradition.

ZEFFIRELLI: I reject this counter-reformist etiquette that Fo is trying to saddle on me. When Fo makes a "life of Christ" he emphasizes pagan joy, and that doesn't seem to me to be the central message of Christianity . . . I am worried about a public that is not accustomed to these kinds of shocks . . . I would like to conclude by encouraging people to read Sermon on the Mount, which is a testament to communal life and reciprocal tolerance . . . What does this have to say when applied to the situation we are discussing? It reminds us that as Christians we don't have to be afraid of anything and we have to accept all challenges. And if anyone finds Dario Fo's performance repugnant, all they have to do is turn off the television or change the channel.

FO: I will conclude by reminding Zeffirelli, and others, of a phrase from the screenplay of *Jesus* by [Carl] Dreyer. The film is never shown, as we all know. One of the disciples of Christ says: "As long as Jesus spoke only to the sages and wise men in the synagogues, no one attacked him, but when he went up onto the mountaintop so that his voice could be heard as far away as possible, and thousands finally could hear him (and I emphasize finally), the authorities began to understand that this was a man to be eliminated as soon as possible."[1]

The 1977 television broadcast of *Mistero Buffo* stirred up controversy throughout Italy. Fo and Rame's one-person reenactments of Bible stories and Church history were denounced in the Vatican newspaper, *L'Osservatore,* as "the most blasphemous program ever broadcast in the history of world television."[2] Fo responded to this criticism with gracious irony: "That is the best compliment the Vatican could have paid me."[3]

Some sources reported that the Vatican considered threatening to break off diplomatic ties with Italy if the state-controlled television station broadcast the second installment of the program. This strategy was rejected, but the Church exerted its political influence with the leaders of the ruling Christian Democratic Party and managed to keep Fo off the national airwaves for the next seven years, a banishment that seemed to be measured in biblical proportions. A re-broadcast of the series that had been scheduled for 1982 was canceled, and a television executive who was a Christian Democrat called Fo "an ideological swindler, a liar, Jacques Tati's mongoloid brother, the true expression of the arrogance of television's power."[4]

After they were barred from television, Fo and Rame continued performing *Mistero Buffo* on stage in Italy and throughout the world. Demand for the performance was so strong that they sometimes staged it in outdoor sports arenas to more than thirty thousand spectators at a time. The 1986 American tour of *Mistero Buffo* played to standing-room audiences and excellent reviews in New York; New Haven; Washington, D.C.; Baltimore and Cambridge. The couple estimates that the work has been seen by more than forty million people worldwide.

Mistero Buffo is the quintessential creation of the Fo/Rame collaboration. The techniques employed in it are key to understanding the theatrical imagination that animates all their work. It is particularly important as an expression of Fo's attempts to reinvent the techniques of the medieval *giullari* for a modern audience. "When I began a long time ago to research the history and origins of the theatre," says Fo, "I realized that most of the early texts were based on religious stories, and that it was impossible to revive the theatre of the giullari without coming to terms with Christianity, its protagonists, and its temporal power. So, little by little, I put together over the years this play that has as its protagonists: Christ, the apostles and the Madonna, and that deals with saints, miracles and the Gospels."[5]

THE MIRACLE OF THE WEDDING AT CANA

Fo's debate with Franco Zeffirelli over the "scurrilous nature" of *Mistero Buffo* was representative of the scandal that surrounded the play's broadcast. It also echoes a scene from the play in which an angel and a drunkard argue over the correct way to tell the story of Jesus turning water into wine during the wedding at Cana. Like Zeffirelli, the angel promotes a conventional view of the Gospels and is scandalized by any suggestion that Christ's miracle might be linked to a Dionysian love of pleasure. Like Fo, the drunkard humanizes Christ by emphasizing his connection to the peasants and their celebrations of fertility, springtime and wine-fueled revelry. The drunkard, who has attended the wedding, rhapsodizes over the wine's sweet fragrance, quoting Christ as saying, "Drink, people! Be happy! Get drunk! Don't wait! Enjoy yourselves!"[6] In the debate, Fo criticized Zeffirelli for leaving this episode out of his filmed life of Christ, arguing that its exclusion promoted the Church's repressive doctrine of urging people to suffer silently in life and wait to enjoy themselves until they get to heaven. For Fo this stands in contrast to the popular peasant tradition that celebrates Christ's resurrection as a continuation of pagan rituals of rebirth that emphasize earthly pleasures.

In the prologue that introduces "The Miracle of the Wedding at Cana," Fo refers to the visual arts to make his point that popular tradition has long linked the figure of Christ to the pagan divinities of Dionysus and Bacchus, the Greek and Roman gods of fertility. Showing his audience a slide of a nineteenth-century engraving called "Palm Sunday," which depicts a Sicilian religious festival, Fo notes that it "depicts three different moments of time in the same situation: the entrance of Christ into Jerusalem (you see, he's the one under the palm branches, surrounded by revelers), Bacchus; and finally the descent of Dionysus into hell. Dionysus is a Greek divinity whose origins can be traced back to Thessalonica fifteen centuries before the birth of Christ. They say he was so enamored of mankind that when a demon kidnapped springtime, to enjoy her all to himself in hell, Dionysus sacrificed himself for humanity by going down to hell on the back of a donkey. He paid with his life so that men could enjoy the spring again. And fifteen centuries later Christ is a god who comes onto the earth to try to give springtime back to man. Springtime is a metaphor for dignity . . . And in the middle is Bacchus, the god of happiness, of drunkenness even, of letting yourself go so that you can be happy."[7]

It is significant that Fo's inspiration comes from an engraving that juxtaposes three cultures into a single image. Regardless of its literal accuracy, this visualization of history resembles the epic vision of narrative that is embedded in all Fo's writing: he conflates time, merges characters and blurs the boundaries between history, fiction, anthropology, politics, religion and slapstick. In *Mistero Buffo*, Fo accomplishes all this alone onstage (he and Rame never appear together in the piece), playing a succession of disparate roles with disarming simplicity. "When I stand here, I'm the angel," he tells the audience at the conclusion of his prologue. "When I stand over there, I'm the drunk. You'll follow it because you're used to watching the news on television."[8] Fo's performance of "The Miracle of the Wedding at Cana" endows the nineteenth-century engraving of Palm Sunday with the immediacy of a contemporary newsreel.

When Fo first performed *Mistero Buffo*, in Milan in 1969, he introduced the monologues by showing slides of artwork ranging from medieval depictions of performing giullari to satirical drawings of the popes. Eventually Fo eliminated the slides, but he continued introducing each piece with a prologue that placed it in historical context. Essentially Fo became the slide show himself, using his voice and gestures to communicate the meanings and forms of the images that had inspired his writing. As years went by, he synthesized the presentation even farther and eventually stopped mentioning the artwork, but his performance of "The Miracle of the Wedding at Cana" continues to embody the spirit of Bacchus, Dionysus, Christ and the revelers surrounding them in the Palm Sunday engraving.

Two other slides that were initially included in the prologue to this scene depicted a close-up of an angel from a fresco by Cimabue and a medieval sketch of a drunkard. The contrasting attitudes of these two images are mirrored in Fo's body language as he depicts the two central characters in his monologue. When he plays the angel he raises his arm in front of his upright body, letting his wrist drop to the same angle used by Cimabue to give the cherub an air of nonchalant tranquility. The angel's near regal detachment is contrasted to the visceral movements of Fo's drunkard, whose slouching postures echo the quirky angles of the souse depicted in the eleventh-century sketch. The drunkard's body throbs with every word he speaks; the angel barely moves, and is annoyed when the drunk keeps interrupting her prim and proper version of the wedding story from which all references to wine have been excised.

"Be quiet, you big drunk," the angel blurts out in a strangled shout, "don't speak."[9] Repressing her exasperation and maintaining a façade of calm, she becomes a comic emblem of censorship, silencing her own feelings at the same time that she muzzles the drunk and attempts to stifle the truth of what happened at the wedding. "I don't want to hear about that drunkenness," she shouts, losing her composure every time the drunk starts talking.[10] She won't let him move a finger, because when he moves, his body makes too much noise. Thinking is also prohibited, because the drunkard's alcohol-soaked brain is also very noisy. By the end, even breathing is forbidden, and the angel threatens to kick her adversary if he doesn't comply.

The drunkard retaliates by pulling out a few of the angel's feathers and threatening to completely deplume her. "I'll pluck you like a chicken," he growls. "Every feather, one by one . . . from your ass too . . . from the rear. Come here, you oversized hen. Come here."[11] The angel flees in terror and the drunk is free to tell his story without interference. It is a bacchanalian tale that depicts Jesus' miracle in vivid detail. The drunk is enraptured as he retraces the path of Christ's wine down his esophagus and into his belly. Then he pantomimes the fragrant aroma returning up his gullet through his nostrils, and wafting in the air so enticingly that a man passing by on horseback is inebriated just by its smell. *"Jesus"* the rider shouts, *"sei di/vino,"* which means both "you are divine" and "you are of wine."[12] The pun is a delicious culmination of the story's Dionysian flavor. Fo embodies both Jesus and the wine, using his gestures to visualize the path of the miraculous liquid through the body of one of Jesus' lowly followers. The scene is a comic inversion of holy communion, foreshadowing the drinking of wine as Christ's blood at the same time that it conjures up pagan visions of the wine gods Dionysus and Bacchus. These densely textured associations are achieved without didactic explication. The sketch itself is structured in the form of a classic circus routine known as the interruption gag, where the austere white-faced clown is frustrated by the ever more annoying interruptions of the goofy august clown. It is the same pattern one finds in the films of Laurel and Hardy or Abbott and Costello, and is immediately accessible to all audiences.

One reason the dialogue between the angel and the drunkard functions so effectively as both slapstick and theological debate is the context in which Fo presents it. The audience may not have heard the argument between Fo and Zeffirelli, but most spectators and readers are familiar with the basic issues that separate Fo's populist interpretation of the Gospels from the doctrine endorsed by the Vatican. By exploring these issues more fully in the comic provocations of his prologue, Fo invites the public into the debate before his story begins, encouraging them to look at the narrative from a multiplicity of viewpoints. When the angel appears, for instance, the audience recalls not only the fresco of Cimabue's angel, but also a Renaissance painting of Jesus at the wedding in Cana that Fo has discussed in his prologue to the story. The painting is by Veronese and Fo acts it out as he describes it, imitating in turn the drunken peasants and their noble patrons, who are shown occupying two different tables. Fo also notes that the painting depicts Christ as one of the aristocrats, removed from the rowdy crowd: "He stays close to the proprietors of the palace with a very aristocratic attitude. He has long fingers, long feet, very fine robes, double-sided . . . as if they were from Scotland . . . almost cashmere." Here, Fo teases his audience with references to contemporary tokens of wealth to make it clear that this is a story with modern implications: "He holds a beautiful goblet . . . wine isn't good enough for him . . . he drinks whiskey!"[13]

Continuing to mock the depiction of Christ as a figure detached from the pain of the world, Fo then refers to a painting by Piero della Francesca. Noting that the painting has recently been stolen from a museum in Urbino and then almost immediately returned to it, he wonders what has happened, and imagines a scene in which a disgruntled thief and an art collector complain about the quality of the work and send it back. Jumping from the present into the world of the painting, Fo imitates the position in which Piero shows Christ: "Very well composed," says Fo, "with his hip tilted. Little clothing, but well covered. Beautiful buttocks. Nicely defined muscles. He's in this position. Note the position." Fo assumes the soft curves of the body shape to show how inappropriate it is for a man being whipped. His hands are joined at the wrists above his head, in a pose of sublime relaxation. Then Fo leaps into the role of the torturer flaying Jesus. A second later he resumes the tranquil pose of Christ, who sighs languidly, "Are you done yet?" Labeling this figure as "completely absent, alienated from suffering, joy and sadness," Fo rejects the vision of Jesus as "lost in a world of ideas, above it all, almost Platonic." He is preparing his audience for the Jesus who will be presented by the drunkard in *Mistero Buffo* as "full of joy, exuberant, someone who, when he is introduced to friends, is the first to have a drink and start singing."[14]

Fo performs the prologue's physical and vocal transformations over the course of a few minutes, taking the audience with startling velocity from ancient Palestine, to medieval Europe, to Renaissance Italy, to heaven, and back to modern times. He even takes time to impersonate the audience in the theatre, enacting the squabbling between a husband and wife who disagree on the politics of his show: "Why did we come here?" says the husband. "You knew these people would be a little to the left," says the wife. "I just came to be exasperated," the man concludes. This improvised diversion grew out of Fo's response to the isolated laugh of a spectator during the television taping of *Mistero Buffo*. Fo later stepped out of character to say he expected Christ's diatribe against the rich to be deleted from the broadcast, and launched into an impersonation of a future television viewer muttering about Fo's audience marching around with red flags and little red books by Chairman Mao.

Fo's polyphonic technique renders his stories far more complex and absorbing than the sum of their plots. By shifting voices swiftly, from Jesus to the drunkard to the Madonna to minor figures in forgotten paintings to angels to scholars to modern politicians to audience members to himself as narrator, Fo activates the public's participation in the ongoing reshaping of the story from each new perspective. Spectators have to leap back and forth between centuries and viewpoints, deciding which side they are on and whom they believe. The confrontation between the drunk and the angel is only one of the main shifting dialogues woven into the performance. By the time these two appear they are sharing the stage with an epic cast drawn from different time periods, each individual triggering a new internal dialogue with the action of the play.

Taking yet another leap through time and theology, Fo muses on the absurdity of presenting Christ as an aristocrat when the Bible provides evidence of Jesus' scorn for the rich. Becoming Christ, Fo yells that it will be harder for a rich man to enter heaven than it would be for a camel to pass through the eye of the needle. Assuming this pronouncement might be a response to overcrowded conditions in heaven, Fo envisions a paradise as crowded as a rush-hour trolley car. He demonstrates the way heaven's residents would have to walk to avoid being poked in the eye by angel wings while they kick tiny cherubim out from under their feet. Next he imagines all the rich people in Palestine trying to squeeze their camels through the eyes of needles. At one point he even becomes a camel, whose hump has been flattened out in the process: "This," he says, "is how the first horse was created." He then hurls himself into a depiction of rich people leading their children in flattening exercises that will enable them to pass through the eye of a needle. They end up walking like Egyptian hieroglyphs, or figures on a Greek vase. Fo demonstrates their two-dimensional movements in a style that parodies Vaslav Nijinsky's famous bas-relief-like choreography for *The Afternoon of a Faun*.

At this point Fo has turned himself into a living hieroglyph. The link between his body and the wall drawings of antiquity becomes part of his comedy. The audience is reminded that all of Fo's texts require the actor to play the role of a human pictograph. His body, or the body of any actor who plays his roles, enters into a dialogue with the spoken text and communicates coded messages to the audience that resonate with multiple meanings. The comic hieroglyph of the rich Palestinian, for instance, in conjuring up associations with Greek vases, is also intended to recall Fo's discussion of Dionysus, who often appears on such vases, and who also appears with Christ in the Sicilian engraving of Palm Sunday that Fo introduced in his prologue. Fo's hieroglyph also provides a precise visual metaphor for the state of detachment from worldly affairs that is satirized in his version of "The Miracle of the Wedding at Cana." The surreal body shape assumed by Fo epitomizes the aloofness depicted in the Renaissance painting of Christ and the Cimabue fresco of the angel. And finally Fo makes a connection to current events by demonstrating the similarity of his hieroglyphic walk to the real-life walk of a modern Italian politician named Ugo LaMalfa, who also acts as if wealth had placed him above the concerns of his working-class constituents.

No spectator will absorb all these associations at once, but by the end of the piece the viewer's head will be swimming with ideas triggered by images of body shapes and gestures, which linger in the memory as vividly as Fo's words. The way Fo pronounces the name "Ugo," for instance, has a pinched nasal condescension that echoes the manner in which he has distorted his facial grimaces to match his flattened-out hieroglyphic walk. The image of snooty condescension conveyed by his face and body is embedded in the haughty tones with which Fo endows the two syllables of the politician's name when he wrinkles his nose and says, "Ewe-go." Fo jokes that LaMalfa changed his name because he could not pronounce the one he was born with through the pursed lips of his flat face.

A similarly dense constellation of ideas is linked to many of the other images in Fo's visual style of writing and performance. The drunkard, ending his account of "The Miracle of the Wedding at Cana," denies that his story is blasphemous, and asserts that if God had taught Adam how to make wine, he would have resisted the temptation of the snake, and we would all still be living in Paradise. This claim is followed by a revisionist version of the story of the Original Sin, in which the drunk plays the part of Adam while his left arm plays the part of the snake slithering up his body and telling him to eat the apple. Instead Adam throws the apple on the ground and takes up a glass of wine. Pouring a few drops on the ground, he makes a toast: "To God, to you, to me, to the earth. Hallelujah."[14] His libation recalls the pagan rituals suggested in the Palm Sunday engraving with which Fo opened his prologue. The toast is accompanied by a sequence of gestures in which Fo raises his glass to the left, to the right, above his head, and then out to the audience. It is almost as if he were forming a cross in the air: his offering to the earth recalls the pagan rituals of Dionysus and Bacchus, antiquity's gods of wine; his reaching out toward the public is a gesture of inclusiveness, linking the present life of the audience to the timeless world of the Gospels; his gesture toward the heavens and his final "Hallelujah" evoke a celebratory sense of spirituality. Taken together, these movements that end Fo's story form a gestural hieroglyph of compassion, fertility, and reverence for life that humanizes Christ at the same time that it brings Fo's inebriated narrator one drink closer to the angels.

MARY UNDER THE CROSS

Mistero Buffo continues to humanize the figures of the Bible with its depiction of the Madonna. In "The Miracle of the Wedding at Cana" the drunk argues that wine cannot be a sin because Jesus offered it to his mother at the wedding. In "The Resurrection of Lazarus" Fo presents Lazarus as a relative deeply mourned by the Madonna, proposing that Jesus performed the miracle "so that he could once again see a smile on the face of his mother."[15]

In the monologue entitled "Mary Under the Cross" Franca Rame plays the part of the Madonna. Depicting Mary as a mother pained by the sight of her son's suffering on the cross, Rame adds a dimension of raw emotion to the play's populist Gospel stories. Her Mary is no saint; she blasphemes against the angel Gabriel and tries to bribe the soldiers to let her climb up and wipe the blood from Christ's mouth. Like Fo, Rame shifts roles swiftly, turning her back to the audience and spreading her arms in a Crucifixion pose to speak in the voice of Christ reassuring his mother that he needs no help. She also gives voice to the bystanders, who try to spare Mary the sight of her son "twisted like the roots of an olive tree gnawed at by ants,"[16] and to the guards, who advise Mary that it is better to let her son die quickly than to comfort him and prolong his pain. The situation between the mother and her dying son becomes real and immediate. The Madonna is seen as a human being, not an icon.

The most startling element of the piece is Mary's anger. As envisioned by Rame, Mary rages against the angel Gabriel when he tries to comfort her—she calls him a charlatan and a fraud for failing to warn her that bearing the child of God would end with her watching her son die a hideous death. Berating him with the fierceness of a woman unjustly wronged, she provokes her audience to imagine an element of the Passion story they may never have considered—the exploitation of a woman by a man whose angelic life in heaven renders him incapable of fully understanding the emotional implications of what he has done: "Turn around and spread your wings, Gabriel," shouts Mary in contempt, "go back to your joyous heaven, which has nothing in common with this wretched Earth, this anguished world. Go, so you don't dirty your finely colored wings . . . Don't you see the mud and blood and cow dung, that it's all a big sewer? Go, so you don't dirty your ears with the desperate shouts and cries and begging that rise up from all directions. Go, so you won't cloud your eyes with the sight of sores, scabs and bubons, and of flies and worms coming out of butchered corpses. You're not used to these things because in heaven there's no noise, no crying, no war, no prison, no hanged men, no raped women. There is no hunger, no famine, no sweat-soaked workers, no babies without smiles, no mothers without hope, no one paying for their sins with pain. Go, Gabriel, go!"[17]

Borrowed from a popular tradition of Passion plays that was familiar to Rame's family of traveling players, this interpretation of Mary's disenchantment reinforces *Mistero Buffo*'s vision of the Gospels as a story of earthly passion. Gabriel is criticized in the same terms Fo has used in his prologue to condemn the Renaissance and medieval paintings that depict Christ as an aloof aristocrat. Rame's fiery performance becomes a hieroglyph of a mother's devotion, a searing portrait that takes the Madonna off the pedestal of conventional religious art and makes her pain as immediate as the suffering of one's next-door neighbor. The emotional truth of Rame's grief-stricken performance establishes *Mistero Buffo* as a play conceived with reverence for Christ's story. At the core of its buffoonery, satire and irony is a deep respect for the misery of a mother and her persecuted son. It reinterprets the Gospels as a challenge to the hardships of an unjust world.

THE RESURRECTION OF LAZARUS

> *What separates an epic clown from an ordinary actor is the quantity of paradoxes that the clown knows how to express through his body, through his voice, through his comic violence.*
>
> —Dario Fo[18]

Fo found his inspiration for "The Resurrection of Lazarus" on the wall of a cemetery in Pisa, where a fresco had faded away to reveal a fragment of the artist's preliminary sketch. "Lazarus wasn't even in it," notes Fo. "Its focus was concentrated on a crowd of spectators, as if they were at the theatre, expressing through gestures their astonishment at the miracle." What intrigued Fo the most, however, was a small detail. "One of the characters was reaching into the purse of a spectator standing near him. He was taking advantage of their astonishment, of their amazement, of the miracle, to steal their money."[19]

Fo builds his version of the Lazarus story around the comic paradox he found painted on the cemetery wall: while the public's attention is turned to heavenly miracles, there will always be someone ready to bring them back to earth by picking their pockets. Beginning with this premise, Fo decided to portray the miracle of Lazarus's resurrection from the point of view of the crowd that came to watch it and the swindlers who try to profit from it. Fo plays over fifteen different roles in the course of his monologue, including the cemetery guardian who sells tickets to the miracle, a fish vendor and gamblers taking odds on the likelihood that Jesus will succeed. There is also a man renting chairs so that people can watch the miracle without fear of fainting from shock and hitting their heads on a tombstone. Any such fatal accidents would be permanent, reminds the huckster in his singsong pitch, because "the saint only performs one miracle a day."[20]

Shifting from one character to another, Fo uses his voice and body to create a cinematic montage that turns the scene of the resurrection into a carnival fairground where onlookers scramble to get a view of the miracle. The arrival of the apostles is greeted with shouts of recognition: "Hey, Mark," yells an excited spectator, proposing that the saint join him for a drink after the miracle. Another viewer complains that he is tired of standing around waiting for the resurrection to begin: "They should have a timetable for these miracles, and stick to it."[21]

When Lazarus actually rises from his tomb, a bystander recounts his shaky first steps with the suspenseful tones of a prize-fight announcer at ringside wondering if a woozy boxer will make it to the next round: "He's rising. He's rising. He's up on his feet. He's falling. He's falling. He's going down. He's going down. He's up. He's down. He's moving forward. He's coming out of the grave like a dog coming out of water. He's shaking himself off. The worms are flying everywhere."[22] At this point Fo uses a film-editing technique to give the audience the illusion that they are watching someone being sprayed by the worms that Lazarus shakes off his partially decomposed body: having pantomimed the action of Lazarus shaking himself "like a dog coming out of water," he shifts position to become an onlooker picking the worms off his chest. "This passage is clear," Fo has written in a post-performance analysis. "One, two, three, I get into position and suddenly reverse the images, or should I say our movie camera changes position. From there it returns to there: a reverse-angle shot in respect to the narrator."[23]

Beginning with a drawing that he reimagines in the form of a film director's storyboard, Fo has written the monologue as a kind of medieval screenplay, articulating his technique in cinematic terms but performing the piece alone onstage as he imagines it would have been performed by a giullare in the Middle Ages. He explains how he moves from a close-up to a wide-angle shot by having the character change the tone of his voice during a crowd scene: "At this instant the situation changes . . . I made it clear that there were people moving around me . . . other spectators who were crowded together and pressing up against my shoulder. Then someone pushes. Note that up until this point the frame of your [the audience's] viewing lens was limited to my face. Then when I pretend to lose my balance the image is enlarged to include the entire stage. I force a change in point of view."[24] Even though there is only one actor onstage, Fo orchestrates the action like a film director handling a cast of hundreds, using a camera to guide the eye of the public to the crucial details of the scene: "If I lower my voice and shrink my gestures, I force you to pay attention and concentrate harder," says Fo, "I almost oblige you to stretch your neck to catch what I have miniaturized. But watch what happens when I execute a big gesture, stretching out my arms . . . I move toward you, turn around and exclaim, 'Who's pushing? Idiot, there's an open grave up here.' Then I make you imagine that the stage space is full of people pushing all around me . . . The tone of annoyance is not raised just to indicate the character is afraid of being pushed into the open grave. The main goal is to make it clear to the audience that the character is talking not only to people close to him but to the crowd that is all around him."[25]

By deftly playing with the focal point of the spectator's attention, Fo builds a relationship with the audience that makes them active partners in shaping the narration. Following his theatrical jump-cuts requires the public to keep thinking about the ideas and moral implications being raised by the changing points of view. This level of audience involvement is an important element in the epic style of theatre championed by Bertolt Brecht. Fo is the most successful contemporary practitioner of Brecht's legacy, and refers often to the principles of epic performance. "Raising and lowering the voice dilates the stage space and physically involves the audience, so that they are transformed into a chorus participating with me onstage. This is the key of epic representation, involving the audience and always keeping them off-balance. The spectator has to be put in the position of being a public witness, conscious of his role, not sprawled out on his seat, passively digesting what he sees."[26]

"The Resurrection of Lazarus," like all of Fo's monologues, was conceived in cinematic terms and written in a language that evokes the gestural equivalent of ever-shifting camera angles. The short phrases, fragmented syntax and paradoxical juxtapositions are intended to activate the metaphoric movie camera that Fo imagines in the eyes of every spectator: "The actor, the director, has to succeed in changing the audience's point of view whenever there is a need. We are accustomed, often without realizing it, to executing incredible zoom effects, focusing on a particular detail, or enlarging the wide panorama of the frame, or stretching things out, or highlighting the shadings of color from the chiaroscuro of the background. In fact we have in our brains a camera that no technical engineer could equal."[27]

The final passage in "The Resurrection of Lazarus" is representative of Fo's cinematic writing technique at its most concise. It depicts the moment Fo found painted on the cemetery wall in Pisa, the moment when the crowd realizes that the miracle of the resurrection is actually taking place before their eyes. "Bravo, Jesus," shouts one of the spectators. "My purse," yells another in alarm, "I've been robbed. Thief!" The instant of the miracle coincides with the instant of the crime, and the body of the actor becomes a virtual metaphor for that paradox by virtue of the three words he repeats as the scene ends. Saying, "Bravo, Jesus," demands that the actor assume a position of reverential awe. A second later his body shifts to a shape of angry frustration as he shouts, "Thief," in an attempt to stop the pickpocket's escape. "Bravo, Jesus" and "Thief!" are repeated three times, pulling the actor's body into two opposing directions as if he were playing both sides of a reverse camera angle in rapid succession.[28] The physical paradox enacted by the actor's muscles parallels the paradox that animates the entire story: pure faith is juxtaposed against crass exploitation. The pickpocketing is seen as a sleight-of-hand deception on par with the profiteering of those who have exploited Christ's miracle as if he were a magician in a carnival sideshow. The parallels to modern-day religious charlatans and television evangelists are obvious, as Fo leaves his audience with the image of a man torn between the sincerity of his beliefs and the realization that his pocket has been picked. The repetition of the two phrases is deceptively simple, but the scenario they express is a complex evocation of paradox in motion.

THE BIRTH OF THE GIULLARE

I am not as interested in politics as I am in justice. What I hope to do is involve the audience in a sense of moral indignation against injustice, not with the theatrical equivalent of political pamphlets, but with entertainments that have a sense of elegance.

—Dario Fo[29]

In Fo's cinematic vision of theatre, the soundtrack is just as important as the camera angles. His texts unfold in rhythmic speech patterns that shrewdly heighten the themes of his stories. A recurring dynamic in Fo's narrative technique is the tension between freedom and oppression. In many of his stories Fo orchestrates the comic climaxes so that they coincide with the victim's liberation, creating a situation in which laughter arises from the defeat of tyranny.

The links between Fo's performance rhythms and his sense of moral indignation emerge clearly in the segment from *Mistero Buffo* entitled "The Birth of the Giullare." It recounts the miracle that gave the first giullare his talent for storytelling.

Fo begins the piece as a traveling player trying to gather a crowd in an open-air piazza. His body whirls through space with the irrepressible energy of a child at a fairground, and he shouts out to his audience in an intoxicating nonstop stream of mixed Italian dialects. Once he wins people's attention, he suddenly stops the cascade of movements and sound, creating a moment of still and intimate eye contact with the public. "I was not always a giullare," he tells them in a confessional tone, "I used to be a peasant, a farmer. But I will tell you how it happened that I became a giullare."[30]

In a series of flashbacks Fo now reenacts the unfair humiliations that the peasant has endured at the hands of corrupt landowners, priests and government bureaucrats. Playing all the characters, Fo vividly conveys the peasant's growing sense of frustration in each new encounter with authority. The priest tries to cheat him out of his land with an oppressive litany of religious double-talk, which Fo builds to an intolerable rhythmic intensity climaxing in the peasant's long-awaited moment of revenge: a good old-fashioned slapstick kick in the buttocks. The same basic patter of oppression, frustration, rage and liberation is repeated in the peasant's encounter with a local notary, but when the landowner and his soldiers rape the peasant's wife, the tone of the piece shifts to a blacker mood of resignation and despair.

As the grief-stricken peasant prepares to hang himself, he is stopped by a gaunt beggar who asks for a drink of water. It turns out to be Jesus, who praises the man for resisting the tyranny of the powerful and counsels him to share his story with others to inspire them to do the same. The peasant argues that his tongue is twisted, his mind is slow and he has no facility with language. In response, Jesus kisses the peasant on the lips, miraculously giving him the gift of telling stories that will move his audiences to laughter and understanding.

Fo performs the moment of the miracle with an exhilarating sense of musicality. As the peasant is transformed by the kiss into a giullare, words spring loose from his mouth like water bursting from a fountain that has been blocked up for years. His arms flow expressively through the air like unbound windmills. The triumph of freedom over tyranny is palpable in each sound and movement. As he viciously satirizes the land-owner with a tongue that now has the power to cut like a knife, it slowly becomes apparent that the piece is ending where it had begun. The giullare is again shouting for the public's attention in the piazza, but now his actions resonate with indignation and the memory of the injustices he has suffered. In "The Birth of the Giullare" as in all of Fo's work, the cadences of the comedy echo the rhythms of revolt.

BONIFACE VIII

> Now we come to Boniface VIII, the pope in the era of Dante. Dante knew him well. He hated him so much that he sent him to hell (in the Inferno) even before he died.
>
> —Dario Fo[31]

In telling the story of the medieval Pope Boniface, Fo uses all the epic theatrical techniques at his disposal, including the creation of a compelling soundtrack, in which the pope sings Gregorian chants, and a modern-day prologue that introduces the story with a portrait of Pope John Paul II. Boniface is seen from a variety of viewpoints, and Fo has compared his narrative strategy of multiple perspectives to the techniques of a sculptor, saying that he circles the story the way a sculptor circles an unfinished statue, examining the way the lights and shadows form when viewed from different directions.[32]

Fo's circling of his stories often begins with a drawing. In one of the first outlines he wrote for *Mistero Buffo* there is a passage that reads, "Boniface sits on a monk. Christ at his feet."[33] This describes a satirical drawing Fo had copied from an early fourteenth-century codex in which Pope Boniface is expressing his disdain for the dissident beliefs of Segalello da Parma by using the monk as a chair. Segalello belonged to a religious order that believed the Church should renounce its earthly possessions and that its representatives should follow Christ's example by living in poverty. The drawing led Fo to create a story about Pope Boniface that stresses the contradiction between the Church's wealth and Christ's poverty.

At the beginning of the piece, Fo communicates this contradiction through the style of the pope's singing. Preparing for a public procession, Boniface sings a Gregorian chant with the aid of the choirboys who help him dress in his finest robes and jewels. Although the solemn rhythms and lofty words of the chant summon up images of spirituality, the pope interrupts the song at irregular intervals to polish his jewels and adjust his luxurious vestments. At one point he pauses for a few beats to clean a mirror with his breath. Then, after admiring himself, the pope resumes the chant with renewed fervor. The rupture of the religious rhythm corresponds perfectly with the collapse of the pope's pious façade.

Boniface's suppression of dissent, which the medieval drawing had shown through the image of the pope sitting on the monk, is expressed by Fo in a recurring comic gesture. Each time the choirboys fail to assist him properly, Fo's pope threatens to hang them by their tongues from the church door—a punishment Boniface is actually said to have imposed on dissident monks. Smiling through gritted teeth, the pope makes his threat with a sly pantomime that begins with the gesture of hammering a nail and ends with the evocation of a body swinging in the breeze as it hangs suspended by a tongue. "Better watch out," warns the pope, with barely suppressed rage that suggests the choirboys will end up squirming in the wind if they don't follow his orders more efficiently.[34] The nail through the tongue is a stark emblem of censorship, and Fo achieves a gruesomely comic effect by repeating it several times in the course of the story, each time with smaller and smaller gestures until it becomes an ironic visual shorthand for the absolute power of the pope, as slapstick hieroglyph of oppression.

The story ends when the pope's procession meets Christ, who is dressed in rags. Boniface is so self-absorbed that he doesn't at first recognize the gaunt and bearded figure, even when the choirboys tell him who it is. When he realizes who is in front of him, he tries to cover up his blunder by blaming the choirboys: "Oh, *that* Jesus," he exclaims, "Jesus Christ! He's got two names. Why don't you use them?"[35]

Fearing that Christ's own renunciation of worldly possessions will make him skeptical of a pontiff dressed in gold and silk, Boniface quickly sheds his robes and jewels and orders the choirboys to cover him with mud. Jesus sees through the charade and gives the pontiff a kick in the tailbone, a blow, according to Fo, that is the origin of the coccyx's Italian nickname as the "sacred bone." Even more humiliating for Boniface is Christ's assertion that he never authorized Saint Peter to establish a papacy in the first place. The pope reacts to the news of his illegitimacy with hysterical silent laughter.[36]

In his prologue to the story, Fo calls the meeting of Jesus and Pope Boniface "a typical anachronism of the Middle Ages." It is the kind of juxtaposition Fo attributes to the medieval giullari, who depicted the pope's actions from Christ's viewpoint to highlight his destructive impact on the present, just as Dante did by writing him into the *Inferno*. Fo adds his own anachronistic elements by juxtaposing the tale of the medieval pope with a story about the 1983 assassination attempt made on the life of Karol Wojtyla, Pope John Paul II. Surprisingly, Fo turns the episode into a comic montage, using his cinematic technique to make the audience feel as if they were watching a documentary newsreel of the event. Fo becomes a crowd waiting for the pope's arrival at the airport. He also becomes the pope's airplane, breaking through the clouds with an oversized papal skullcap on its cockpit, as well as an onlooker, who believes the pope himself is flying and has to be reminded, "No that's not him. The pope's inside . . . The pope doesn't have little windows."[37]

The theme of censorship appears in the prologue when Fo describes the pope tripping down the stairs from the plane to the runway: "No one knows how to go down stairs more quickly than the pope," says Fo, using the flapping of his hands to create a close-up of the pope's feet fluttering down a staircase. "The only problem was, he didn't see the last ten steps." Fo then shows how the fall is censored by the television cameras transmitting the event on a delayed broadcast: he shows the pope beginning to go down the steps, then depicts the pope dusting himself off after a jump-cut in the tape that eliminates the fall completely.[38]

Fo's reenactment of modern media censorship in the prologue echoes the graphic tongue-piercing threat of censorship that is at the heart of his portrait of Boniface. The audience is reminded that the medieval story has modern resonance, a resonance made even more immediate by the fact that the play they are watching was actually censored by the Vatican, whose newspaper accused it of "encouraging the complete disintegration of Italian society."[39] Fo added the modern version of the prologue after the play had been banned, under Vatican pressure, from the national television stations, which were controlled by the Christian Democratic Party. The prologue reinforces the prismatic nature of the performance, encouraging audiences to reevaluate the relationship between politics and religion from multiple perspectives, ranging from television broadcasts of the pope to the threat of a nail through the tongue.

THE QUINTESSENTIAL GIULLARE

If there is a single work that embodies the essence of Fo and Rame's theatrical artistry, it is *Mistero Buffo*. Their masterpiece, the play provides the techniques that animate all their theatre. Every monologue is infused with the rhythmic drive of a jazz improvisation, the immediacy of a newspaper headline and the epic scope of a historical novel. Like all their work, *Mistero Buffo* elicits a multiplicity of overlapping dialogues: between the actor and the audience; between the text and the body of the actor; between conventional visions of the Bible and provocative reinterpretations of the Gospels; between the visual sources of the play and the text they inspired; and between standard uses of language and the invented dialect with which the stories are told. The literal meaning of *Mistero Buffo* is "comic mystery play." The mystery plays were sacred representations performed in the Middle Ages. Going back to those medieval source materials, Fo created a virtuosic work that established him as a modern-day giullare. He has continued to perform *Mistero Buffo* throughout his career, and returns to its biblical themes in numerous other works, including a collection of monologues entitled *The Peasants' Bible* (1996). Always respectful of the populist versions of Christ's story, Fo chose to tell it the way he imagined it had been preserved through the oral tradition of the medieval giullari, and through the paintings and frescos of their contemporaries.

In my research on medieval texts I encountered, too often to ignore, this figure of Christ transformed by the people into a kind of hero in opposition to authority, and to the hierarchy of the Church, which had always tried to monopolize him and keep him distant from the people. It should be remembered that until well after the year 1000 people were prohibited from reading the Gospels, and that their translation into the vernacular took place very late. Yet the people did not accept their exclusion and had given life to a vast number of Apocryphal Gospels, from which a different Christ emerged. He was more human and always on the side of the weakest. He had in him a pagan, almost Dionysian joy for love, feasting, beauty and earthly things. And at the same time he was full of hatred and violence toward hypocritical priests, the aristocracy who wanted to dominate the weak, and a triumphant Church and its temporal power. This is probably not the historical Christ, but it is the Christ who was created by the vast culture of the popular tradition.

—Dario Fo[40]

ENDNOTES

1. Dario Fo and Franco Zeffirelli, debate in *La Repubblica* (Milan), April 27, 1977. From the Fo/Rame archive in Milan.
2. *L'Osservatore* (Rome), April 24, 1977. Quoted by Tom Behan in *Dario Fo: Revolutionary Theatre* (London: Pluto, 2000), p. 102.
3. Fo, in *La Repubblica* (Milan), April 25, 1977. Quoted by Tom Behan, in *Dario Fo: Revolutionary Theatre*.
4. Quoted by Behan, in *Dario Fo: Revolutionary Theatre*, p. 102.
5. Fo, in *Panorama*, April 26, 1977. Quoted by Chiara Valentini, in *La Storia di Dario Fo* (Milan: Feltrinelli, 1977), p. 176. Parts of the quotation also appear in Behan, *Dario Fo: Revolutionary Theatre*, p. 102, and Tony Mitchell, *File on Fo* (London: Methuen, 1989), p. 100.
6. Fo, *Mistero Buffo* (Turin: Einaudi, 1977), p. 66.
7. Ibid., pp. 53–54.
8. Fo, *Mistero Buffo*, in the televised version broadcast on RAI Italian National Television in 1977.
9. Fo, *Mistero Buffo*, p. 58.
10. Ibid., p. 62.

11. Ibid.

12. Ibid., p. 64.

13. This quotation and all others from the prologue to "The Miracle of the Wedding at Cana" are taken from the televised version of *Mistero Buffo* broadcast by RAI. Later versions of the prologue do not always include these detailed discussions of artworks, but the early prologues are valuable in illuminating the visual sources at the root of Fo's creative process.

14. Fo, *Mistero Buffo*, in the televised version broadcast by RAI.

15. Ibid.

16. Fo, *Mistero Buffo*, p. 160.

17. Ibid., p. 168

18. Fo quoted in Ron Jenkins, "Clowns, Politics and Miracles," *American Theatre*, June 1986, p. 16.

19. Fo, *Mistero Buffo*, p. 97.

20. Ibid., p. 100.

21. Ibid.

22. Fo, in a televised version of "The Resurrection of Lazarus" broadcast by RAI as part of Fo's lecture/demonstration "The Tricks of the Trade," 1985.

23. Fo, *Manuale minimo dell'attore* (Turin: Einaudi, 1987), p. 155.

24. Ibid., p. 146

25. Ibid.

26. Ibid., p. 147.

27. Ibid., p. 146.

28. Fo, *Mistero Buffo*, p. 104.

29. Fo, quoted in Jenkins, "Clowns, Politics and Miracles," p. 14.

30. Fo, *Mistero Buffo*, p. 72.

31. Ibid., p. 105.

32. Fo, interview with the author, Milan, July 2, 1999.

33. Fo, quoted in Marisa Pizza, *Il Gesto, la parola, l'azione: Poetica, drammaturgia e storia dei monologhi di Dario Fo* (Rome: Bulzoni, 1996), p. 221.

34. Fo, *Mistero Buffo*, p. 116.

35. Fo, from a tape of "Boniface VIII" in performance at the Joyce Theater, New York, June 4, 1986.

36. Ibid.

37. Ibid.

38. Ibid.

39. Behan, *Dario Fo: Revolutionary Theatre*, p. 102.

40. Fo, in *Panorama*, April 26th, 1977, quoted by Valentini, in *La Storia di Dario Fo*, pp. 176–77.

Reprinted from *Artful Laughter: Dario Fo and Franca Rame*, Aperture Press, New York, 2001.

MISTERO
BUFFO

TRANSLATOR'S NOTE

The following pieces were written by Dario Fo and edited by his artistic and life partner, Franca Rame. They are based on fragments of medieval and Renaissance texts that have been reimagined by Fo as scripts that might have been performed by medieval "giullari," itinerant storytellers and satirists who countered official church Gospels with tales that grew out of the oral and pictorial folk tradition of religious stories. Fo believes that the giullari were the artistic ancestors of Harlequin and other characters of the commedia dell'arte. In Fo's prologues to these "giullarata" (performance texts for giullari) he sometimes refers to slides and documentation that were part of his original performances. These references are included in the definitive Italian version of the play as edited by Franca Rame, and are included here to give the reader a sense of Fo's ongoing dialogue with his audience.

—Ron Jenkins

AUTHOR'S NOTE

"Mistero" is a term that has been used since the times of the ancient Greeks in reference to sacred representations enacted by esoteric cults: the Eleusinian and Dionysian mysteries. The term was later used by Christians to describe their rituals up until the third and fourth centuries after Christ. Still today, in churches one occasionally hears the priest declaim: "In the first glorious mystery . . . in the second mystery . . ." and so on. In the Middle Ages "mystery" acquired the simple meaning of sacred representation; "mistero buffo" therefore refers to the representation of sacred themes from a grotesque and satiric point of view. But it should be understood that the "giullari," the popular comic actors of the Middle Ages, were not trying to mock religion, God and the saints, but attempted instead to unmask and denounce in a comic key the shrewd maneuvering of those who exploited religion and things sacred for their own personal benefit.

Ever since the first centuries after Christ, on the occasion of certain rites, particularly those related to Easter, like the "Risus Pascalis," the faithful, under the supervision of the giullari or priests, with especially good senses of humor, entertained themselves by staging grotesquely ironic spectacles, precisely because the theatre, and the comic theatre, in particular, has always been a primary means for people to express, communicate, and even provoke and get worked-up about their ideas. The theatre was the speaking and dramatized newspaper of the so-called "lower classes."

—Dario Fo

THE BIRTH OF THE GIULLARE

PROLOGUE

This is a text in the style of Ragusa, collected in the nineteenth century by a friend and collaborator of Pitrè, the famous scholar from
Palermo who published an incredible mass of documentation
about the popular traditions of Sicily. Later some fragments fell
into my hands, which were from stories on the same theme that
were performed by giullari in northern Italy, in Cremona to be
exact. I grafted some of these fragments into the text from Ragusa
and gave birth to the "tale" that I'm going to present to you. It can
be seen as an almost autobiographical text about a giullare who
tells how he chose to become a storyteller of the people, performing outdoors in the marketplaces to entertain and provoke the
public. As his opening pitch the giullare promises that his jokes
and gags will succeed in making everyone laugh so hard that actual
miracles will ensue—a hunchback will immediately laugh himself
straight, his chest thrust out and his back flat as a board; a woman
who has stopped lactating will see her tits suddenly engorged
with so much milk that it will start spraying out of her nipples like
a fountain.

The giullare's speechifying seems unstoppable, when all of a
sudden, he changes tone, and decides to talk about himself and his
origins: "I was a peasant," he began, "I had no intention of choosing
this profession. I was in no way cut out for it." And then he reveals a
truly incredible twist of fate—he assures us that he was convinced
to take up the profession of clowning by Christ himself. "Being a
peasant is truly difficult," the giullare assures us, "especially when

7

you're working under a master on land that doesn't belong to you. I worked from dawn to evening, and every day the first water the ground drank was my sweat."

But one day, climbing a hill, he discovered almost by chance a rocky piece of land that was uncultivated and didn't belong to anyone. Helped by his wife and children, he cleared the new land and found water to irrigate it. At this point a priest and a notary (maybe a lawyer) introduce themselves to him one after the other . . . both reclaiming possession of the land on the mountain in the name of the owner of the entire valley. He, decisive and confident, chases them away. But in the end the landowner himself arrives, and with great arrogance, heatedly demands the restitution of the land. The peasant resists and blocks him. The landowner then attacks and has him beaten by his henchmen, and then, before the peasant's eyes, he rapes his wife, who goes mad, and then leaves him; the house and the crops are burnt. Defeated and humiliated, the peasant decides to hang himself from the last beam that remains in place between the burnt-out walls, when suddenly three emaciated beggars appear before him asking for water. One of them is Jesus who speaks to the peasant, almost attacking him. He gives him a true and honest lesson on the human condition, speaking about the just punishment that will be received by those who choose to live for themselves so that they don't have to share their fortunes and privileges with the desperate people of his race. In the end, he teaches him the use of gestures and words that will give him faith in himself and in others like him, who are also oppressed and mistreated.

But this is a discourse that is better heard directly in its entirety and in the original language.[1]

———

GIULLARE: Ahh . . . come, people . . . the giullare is here! The giullare, that's me . . . can leap into the air and talk like crazy and . . . *(Executes a comic pirouette)* See, I made you laugh! Come, and I'll make you laugh till you pee in your pants . . . you'll die laughing when I show you that all you

1. Fo originally performed *Mistero Buffo* in a dialect he invented to approximate the medieval vernacular of the giullari.

have to do to aristocrats who go around all smug and puffed-up like balloons when they make war and commit butchery . . . is to uncork them, pull out the stopper in their ass and—PFFF!!—they deflate and burst open like blisters!

Come here . . . it's the time and the place for me to play the clown for you! Everybody gather 'round me! Come! I'll teach you a new way to be in the world. Come . . . come! Watch the gags and the falls that I'll improvise for you . . . a little song, and I can even do it in falsetto hopping on one foot!

Look at my tongue, how it spins! Ah . . . ah . . . it's a windmill, a knife . . . I'll show you how to transform words into razor blades that hack off the heels of lying imposters. But first I'll tell you how I got funny enough to make people laugh till they pee in their pants. Because I wasn't born from a lightning bolt that fell from the sky—e, op!—here I am: "Good morning, good evening!" No, I, in all modesty, am a living miracle! You don't want to believe me?

Yes, it's true. I was born a peasant. With my hoe in the sod. I didn't have much to be happy about: I didn't have land. I didn't have anything!

The only thing I could do to earn a living was to indenture myself to a master: bend over and tire myself out with backbreaking work.

You have to believe me . . . listen to me!

No, it is not by chance that I jumped up on a platform to make you snicker . . . No, my mother didn't just look at her baby sprawled out in the cradle laughing his head off and shout: "What a cute pretty little face you have . . . you make me happy! Little laughing buffoon! Listen, when you grow up, I'm going to make you a giullare!"

No! And I didn't just happen to see my reflection at the bottom of a shiny pan that I used for a mirror and say: "Oh, what joyous sparkling eyes that spread the light of happiness to all places. I'm such a splendidly nice guy! I'm going to be a giullare!"

And it didn't just happen that God the Father, who's always spying out from behind the clouds—since he hasn't got anything better to do—meditated on his blessed creation and shouted: "Oh, what a beautiful world I gave birth to! Oh, what beautiful trees I planted!" *(Changes tone)* "And what's that? It's a peasant! What a face he's got! Nice looking! Eh, peasant. Drop the shovel, give up the land, go be a clown, and don't bust my balls!"

No, no, it wasn't him! It was his son Jesus.

A miracle!

I'm not kidding, I swear it! A miracle made by him himself, Jesus Christ in person. He was the one who transformed me into a giullare!

You don't believe me? That's clear. Then I'm going to show you! Okay?

Every morning I got up when it was still dark . . . the sun hadn't risen yet and I was already curved over my hoe pounding and beating the sod: my sweat was the first water the earth drank.

In the evening I came home drunk . . . dead tired, my eyes bleached by the light and I didn't even want to play with my babies . . . or play love games with my girl . . . my wife . . . I stretched myself out exhausted on the bed . . . a bed of straw . . . and went to sleep. No, I didn't fall asleep! I fainted! And in the night my sleep had no dreams.

Cocka-doodle-doo!

Dammit! I have to exhaust myself all over again!

But one day I went back to the field by way of a riverbank where I looked for some crabs . . . I lost my way and, all of a sudden, I found myself in front of a black mountain that I didn't recognize.

Amazing! High!

And I asked a man going by with a cart: "Friend, who does it belong to, this boastful mountain that shoots up to the sky out of nowhere?"

"To nobody."

"But how can a huge mountain like this not belong to anybody?"

"It's worthless. It's black stone belched up from a volcano. We call it: 'the devil's shit-heap.'"

"It must have given the devil a big pain in the ass when he squeezed this pile of shit out of his butt."

And I went up there . . . climbing on my hands and knees and scratching my nails between the crevices of the stone . . . I dug up a handful of earth . . . I sniffed it: sweet, rich! I went down, running all the way home to my wife. I called to her from the courtyard, shouting with happiness . . . she grabbed a hoe and bucket and came alongside me with the children.

Once we got to the top of the hill, without even taking a breath, we began to hoe the ground everywhere, digging up what little earth there was and then we went down to the riverbank to collect the earth in small buckets. We even went to the cemetery; we stole dirt from the dead. (The earth under old coffins is beautiful! Rich!) And we carried it up by the bucketful and spread out this dung-filled earth: day after day, we laid it out in terraces . . . a stairway of terraces.

Everybody worked, even the children.

Happily!

And my wife, beautiful, pale-skinned . . . she balanced baskets of earth on her head. She moved upright like a queen. Sparkling eyes, full firm breasts . . . so that when she came running towards you, they swayed like fruit in the wind. Oh . . . So beautiful! My sweet love!

And she sang! She sang so purely that her voice arrived directly in your mind.

Day after day, moon after moon, we built up so many terraces that it looked like the Tower of Babel!

But there was no water . . .

With metal pikes we dug holes for wells, but not a drop sputtered out. We had to go down to the river, descending and climbing back up, all of us, the wife and children too, with buckets and buckets, but the dryness always came back: this earth drank as if there was a thirsty dragon underneath it!

One day I went to the top of the mountain with a pick on my shoulder and cursed: "Damn you, God!" And full of rage I gave the pick a big kick into the stone—PIUM!— The stone split open and—SVUOOOM! SCCIHUUUM!— And out of the ground came a huge gusher of water that nearly drowned me.

"Oh Lord . . . thank you! I guess you have to curse to get you to make miracles, Holy God!"

Geysers of water were shooting up everywhere . . . And it went gurgling down the hillside flooding all the land!

My wife burst into tears with a cry of joy and the children splashed around in the mud like fish in heat!

"Thank you! Thank you, God!"

A sweet aroma spread all over . . . it was the grass that came up right away! I planted a seed of rye. No sooner had I turned around then—TACK!—the bud of a leaf shot up!

The earth was golden!

One night I forgot my hoe and left it stuck in the ground. The next morning I came back and it was full of flowers: a flowered hoe!

Fruit burst out of the trees . . . birds came to make their nests . . . the aromas . . . the grain, the wheat . . . Oh! What madness! I was terrified I would wake up and find it had been a dream.

I went to meet the rose-colored sky, when the sun was sinking behind the mountains, and I said: "God! I know . . . I know you're always there inside the sun in moments like this and I thank you for the bountiful gifts that you have granted me with this miracle! I will be grateful . . . even at the cost of my blood, I will turn this earth into heaven on earth for you. Amen!"

When I passed by my fellow peasants they said: "His ass is lucky! He turned a dry mountain into a Garden of Eden." And they were jealous.

I was working in the field when I turned my head and caught sight of the owner of the entire valley. He was on his horse, headed towards me. He cast his eyes around and looked at me . . . and then he spoke to me brusquely: "Who's responsible for this miracle? Who made this land burst into flower?"

"Me, sir! Me. I did it . . . I carried the earth lump by lump . . . I sculpted the terraces . . . Me! Even the water, it wasn't there before . . . I made it gush out with a hoe! This mountain that belonged to no one is mine!"

"Belonging to no one is a phrase that doesn't exist. Here, if you don't know, the entire valley, even the river, the land the stones, everything . . . has an owner. And I'm the one who owns it! I even own the air you're breathing."

"But I asked around . . . they called this hill the shit-heap of the devil because no one ever wanted it. Not even you, Landowner."

"Maybe that was true . . . at one time . . . but now I've changed my mind: It's mine!"

He snorted a laugh and left. Kicking his spurs into the horse, he disappeared!

A few days later I caught sight in the distance of the priest, who was climbing up the incline all dressed in black, sweating and using his handkerchief to mop up the sweat that was dripping down from his forehead to his neck . . . And already from a distance he was shouting: *(In gibberish based on Latin)* "Peasant, dear farmer, in pax vobiscum I come to pray that you vanquish your pride and presumption in cogito ergo sum that this property belongs to you dominus pacem heaven forbid. No one but the pope, Holy Father, ex libro and the emperor adeste fideles can decide who is master of the land habeas corpus, and they have decided, my son, sanctus, sanctus, that you have to give it to the landowner, pax domini, padre spiritus sanctus, ipso facto, hallelujah."

When he got close I whacked him with my hoe, him and the ass he was riding! You never saw somersaults performed with such speed: he kicked his heels into the donkey's balls, and went bouncing hippity-hoppity all the way down the hill, cursing so furiously that he made me cross myself!

Two days later a notary showed up with a big fat mule with a fat ass . . . The notary had a fat ass too, so fat that when he got out of the saddle you couldn't tell if it was his ass that was coming down or the mule's!

He unfurled a long, dark parchment covered with signs, curlicues and crosses and read it without taking a breath, spitting out the words like a litany: "My dear

13

friend, I well understand, and grant you proud cognizance of the fact that it was unknown to the common people that this hill belonged to anyone, but casting a glance at this piece of antique parchment, one can clearly see that this land was in the possession of King Bozo the First, who gave half his territory beyond the river to one of his lovers . . . A holy nun, and the other half to a bastard son, the most beloved of all the bastards he sired. But it so happened that in those times the banks of the river were flooded by a storm that divided it into two streams, half on one side and half on the other, leaving in the middle an island on which stood a black hill. Because of this, for centuries the hill was not claimed by anyone. But today our noble landowner has discovered the occurrence of this river flood and rightfully demands the return to his possession of this diabolical shit-heap!"

The notary did not have time to take a breath before I let loose a big wallop, a bite on the buttocks, and off he was in a gallop, him and his mule!

"This land is like a part of my arm! I won't give it up to anyone!"

But then came the day that the landowner appeared with his henchmen.

We were in the fields working, with the children, my wife . . . and his soldiers grabbed me, stretched out my arms and held me so I couldn't move. The landowner dropped his pants, took my wife and hurled her to the ground: he ripped off her dress, opened her legs and jumped onto her. He mounted her like she was a cow. And all the soldiers laughed.

The children looked at me with wide eyes . . . the color drained out of them. They looked at their mother . . . they looked at me.

And I struggled . . . I succeeded in freeing myself; I grabbed a hoe and shouted: "Miserable wretch! Take this!"

"Stop, child! Stop!" my wife shouted at me. "Don't give them a pretext for killing you. That's what they're waiting for. You rightly think that it's better to die than to tarnish your honor . . . but you have no honor. Honor belongs only to those who possess things, money, land! We who are stripped of everything have no honor! Our honor is the earth! Save the earth, hold on to the earth and spit on your honor!"

And suddenly I lost all my will . . . I dropped the hoe onto the ground.

The soldiers snickered and growled: "Cuckold, asshole without dignity! They mounted his woman and he stands there gawking like a fool!"

The landowner got back onto his horse and his hench-man followed behind on foot.

"Now you can keep your precious land. You paid me well for it." And he laughed.

Moving like a dazed herd of animals we went back to our house.

My wife led the way, in front of us all. She didn't look at anyone.

My children didn't look at me.

I didn't look at them.

No one looked at anyone.

When my wife went into town to get supplies for the house, the people on the road avoided her. No one said good morning . . . as if no one had seen her.

After a few nights my wife ran out of the house screaming, fleeing towards the mountain . . . laughing as she climbed . . . clapping her hands, singing shameless songs at the top of her lungs.

She was insane.

"Stop! Don't do that, my sweetness! Come back to your senses . . . it doesn't matter to me . . . you'll always be my love!"

She didn't answer me. She disappeared. I never saw her again.

The children stopped speaking. They didn't play. They didn't laugh. They didn't cry.

Day after day they wasted away. They died! One after the other, they died!

I was the only one left . . . the only Christian on the scorched earth . . . since the soldiers had burned the house and the woods.

Dumbfounded, I didn't know what to do. One evening I took a piece of rope, threw it over a beam, the last one remaining between the smoldering walls . . . I made a knot, put it around my neck and said: "God, who even in the dark of night watches men by the light of thousands of stars, what accursed game were you playing when you gave me the gift of land and the water, filling me with hope . . . and then right away sending me back into the shit of despair? You have to tell me if you were using a red hot iron to brand me as a clear example that anyone who begins life as a poor peasant, will always stay one . . . and should never presume to have any hope or dreams! Lord, I tell you that it was a huge cruel joke to let me taste heaven on earth and then blow raspberries at me and throw me down into hell without pity! And then I want to tell you that I would like to return to you this life of shit that you have given to me. Take back this life!"

Just when I was about to jump and hang myself, I felt a hand resting here on my shoulder. I turned and it was a young man with long hair . . . shabby . . . a pale face . . . big eyes, sweet and sad, who said to me: "Could I have a little water to drink. I'm thirsty?"

"What kind of time is this to ask for a drink, just when a man is trying to hang himself? Don't you have any manners?"

He cast a glance . . . he had a pitiful look about him, like a man bearing a cross. Near him stood two other wretches: one with white hair and a long white beard and the other clean-shaven . . . thin and smooth as if he had been washed in lime . . . with a haggard face.

"Is there anything else you all would like to drink! Maybe something to eat while you're at it!" *(He makes a gesture of removing the noose from his neck)* "All right, I'll give you a little something to eat and then I'll hang myself!"

I go . . . and look under the last arch still standing. I found some beans and two onions. I boiled them. I filled three bowls and passed them out. They ate ravenously like starving men. Then when they had sated their hunger, the youth with the thin figure and big eyes smiled at me and said: "Thanks for the hot soup! Do you have any idea who I might be?"

I looked at him closely: "It seems to me that you . . . could almost be . . . Jesus Christ!"

"Good! You guessed it! This is Paul and that's Peter."

(He bows his head as a sign of respect) "Pleasure to meet you! Is there anything else I can do for you?"

"What you've given us is enough. I know you, Farmer, I know what happened to you . . . what you've done . . . I know the suffering it cost you to cultivate this land, to make blossom this mountain squeezed out of the devil's buttocks. I know about the sweat of your wife and children . . . and of the landowner's violence against your woman. All for the pride of not leaving this land. Great strength and courage . . . you have proven yourself a good man! But it is just that you come to this end . . . in this manner."

(In a resentful tone) "Why, Christ?"

"Because you kept everything only for the land and didn't share anything with the other peasants, who are as poor as you!"

"But what are you saying? Share with others this scrap of land that wasn't even enough for me and my family?"

"Don't be a whiner . . . many others, as desperate as you, could have done what you did! Tell me, Peasant . . . did you go around visiting the farmhouses . . . and the huts of straw to tell your story? Have you tried to involve them in your life? No? All right then, from now on you have to do something so that others can benefit from what has happened to you . . . you have to tell them about the landowner . . . about the heinous thing he did to your wife and, before that, about the priest and the notary! And then listen to what they tell you. And don't recount each thing whiningly, but with a chuckle . . . teach them to laugh! Transform even terror into laughter. Take the chiselers who try to cheat you with their endless babbling

and turn them upside down with their asses in the air! . . .
And let everyone mock them with belly laughs . . . so that
the laughter will melt all their fears!"

"But I don't know how, I don't know how to turn words
around . . . I don't know how to make mockery . . . Even
nursery rhymes and children's riddles make my tongue
trip on my teeth . . . my brain has been fried by the sun
and exhaustion!"

"You're right. It will take a miracle!"

He took my head in his hands . . . he held me close to
his face and said: "I, Jesus Christ, will this moment give
you a kiss on the mouth and you will feel your tongue
whirling like a corkscrew and then it will become like a
knife that cuts and slashes . . . shaping words and phrases
as clear as the Gospels. And then you will run into the
piazza! You will be a giullare! You'll pull down the
landowner's pants. You'll make the soldiers, priests and
notaries turn white, exposing themselves as naked as
worms!"

And just like that he took my head, put his sweet lips
against mine and kissed me. A wisp of flame touched my
lips . . . my tongue began to trill and twist like a water
snake. New words wiggled and rolled around inside my
brain. Every thought turned itself over . . . every idea
came out upside down.

I ran breathlessly down into the town, and jumped
onto the steps of the baptistery and shouted: "Hey, people! The giullare is here! Come and listen . . . pay attention! I'll show you how to transform words into razor-
sharp blades that instantly slit the throats of infamous
imposters . . . and other words that become drums to
wake up sleeping minds! Come! Come, people! Come!"

on gives your horse

s that once swarmed

the putrid peasants

rk, put a stiff tax on it.
quat, put the same tax

l sing songs that are

e themselves happy.
easures, or else they

rpose on earth is to

t bit, and catch rabies
they come down with

les to sleep
to the sheep.
g an eye
nearby.
gry, that your flock he

will never be missed.
elds, to weed your tall

cted by the weeds of

d-given duties
sing young beauties.
em to you instead
dance in your bed.
her roll 'round in your

nice country wedding
ge 'neath her gown like

THE BIRTH OF THE PEASANT

In the slide now being projected there is a representation of an angel with unfolded wings on the right side, who is entrusting to his master a newly created servant, a battered peasant leaning on a thick staff.

This miniature reminds us of a famous story told by giullari, the text of which was rediscovered in a publication that dealt with the poetic-satiric origins of the Italian vernacular. The author of this text is known as Matazzone or Mattazzone, Mattacchione from Calignano or from Carignano, a little town in the province of Pavia. Concerning the time in which it was written and certainly performed, some researchers place the date in the thirteenth century, others in the fifteenth. The monologue is written in a crude Lombardi dialect, full of terms from a rustic environment, with a vocabulary that is particular to the countryside. The tale begins with the lamentation of a man, the son of Adam, who reminds God that He promised to provide help and a reduction of suffering after the passing of seven generations: "Lord, I can't go on! Your punishment has been truly severe: working on the land has ravaged me, and my wife is getting old before her time. You promised that after the passing of seven generations, you would grant me a little help!"

And the Heavenly Father: "And wasn't it a help when I gave you the donkey to carry all the sacks, the oxen to pull the plows, the horse to put between the poles of your carts?"

"Yes," responded the man. "But it's always up to me to push the plow, lift up the sacks and lead the horse. I'm asking for some-

one who can substitute for me in these labors, so I can [
of things, enjoy the fruits of his labor and rest!"

"Oh, I understand—you want a peasant."

"What is a peasant?"

"If I haven't created one yet, how can you know
Come . . . let's put one in the world . . . let's go see Adam.

When Adam saw the Heavenly Father arriving acc
by a man, he immediately suspected that He wanted
from him, so he put his hands on his chest and shout
enough, Lord! I'm not giving up any more ribs . . . I alreac
share with the birth of Eve!"

"Look, that's fine, you're right," admitted the Heave
"but now what am I going to do?"

At that moment a donkey passed by and an idea ca
Heavenly Father like a thunderbolt—because when it
ideas he is a regular volcano! He made a gesture putting
on the belly of the donkey, and all of a sudden it expand
pregnant.

Now I will perform the text in the Lombardi verna
giullare is Matazzone da Calignano, but I have allowed m
liberty of enriching the original story by inserting
grotesque passages found in Bescapè and Bonvesin de la
seasoned it with sayings and proverbs from the popular I
tradition and medieval songs.

I begin at the moment in which the Lord catches sigl
donkey and makes it pregnant.

━━━

GIULLARE: At that moment, you can imagine it yours
    donkey passed by, ambling around, and the H
    Father was inspired, struck by an idea like light
    because when it comes to ideas he is a regular v
    He raised his hand over the hefty beast and—TR/
    in a flash, the donkey's belly was all puffed-up. In
    to speak frankly, it was pregnant.

Nine months went by . . . the big belly of the bea
ready to explode . . . you could hear a lot of rumblin
donkey let loose a tremendous fart and along v
popped out a stinking peasant.

Because you'll find his conditi
    some advantages
The beast will be free of the flie
    'round his head
For the flies will be plaguing
    instead.
Whatever they earn from their wo
And when they stop working to s
    on their shit.
At carnival, let them dance an
    snappy
So for a few hours they can mak
But not too much of those pl
    might stop
Remembering that their sole p
    work till they drop.
In March let them go barefoot, ge
And keep tending the vines till
    scabies.
In April put them out in the stal
So they can lie down right next
Tell them to sleep without closi
For the ravenous wolf is lurking
And when the wolf gets so hur
    cannot resist
Let him feed on a peasant, who
In May send him out to the fi
    grasses
But make sure he's not distr
    young lasses
For it is one of the peasant's G
To renounce any interest in ch
One at a time he should send t
So you can have fun when the)
Then when you tire of having
    bedding
Marry her off to a peasant in a
Where the bride's belly will bu
    a bubble

And the peasant can thank you for saving him the trouble.
In June send him up to the treetops to take his chances
Collecting baskets of fruit from the trees' highest
    branches.
But to keep him from eating the best peaches and nuts
First feed him plenty of bran bread to plug up his guts.
In July and August, when the heat makes your head
    burst
Give him vinegar and salt water to quench his dry thirst.
And if he curses 'gainst God, fear not for his ill-born
    soul's sin
For whether he's good or he's bad, hell's the place he'll
    end up in.
In the month of September, when the harvest is ample
Give him bunches of grapes on which he can trample.
You can make him a gift of the stalks from the vine
But first make him drain out all the head-spinning
    wine.
In October be sure that the peasant remembers
To butcher your pigs till each one's dismembered.
You can leave him the guts as a sweet treat to eat
But not all, since you'll need some to make your
    sausages sweet.
From the blood of the pig let him drink satisfaction
Since its poison will give him a toxic reaction.
Give lots of fat ham to the peasant to please him
But only to salt it and make it well seasoned.
Then force him to haul it on his back like a beast
To your table where it will make a fine feast.
In November and December when the cold makes him
    shiver
Send him hunting for firewood down by the river
And when he has finished chopping your fuel
Make him carry it to you on his back like a mule.
If he comes close to your fire to make himself warm
Send him outside to go stand in the storm.
And if water pours down from the sky helter-skelter
Send him off to the churchyard to find himself shelter.
He can pray there, say mass, and sing sacred ditties

But none of his prayers will bring him much pity
For although salvation is his ultimate goal
He's doomed not to find it, for he hasn't a soul.
This mule-born peasant's had no proper christening
So why does he think that God will be listening.
He wasn't born to a woman, it was only an ass
And what's more, the poor donkey was just passing gas.

The sarcastic allusion to the origin of the master that defines the peasant as one without a soul and therefore more like an animal than a human, brings to mind another character that was born in the popular imagination, and that is the wild man: a kind of uncontrollable troglodyte that we find among the masked characters of carnival, in farces performed in the Middle Ages, both in the country-side and in the city, an invention of the common people.

The comic *homo selvaticus* (wild man) was noted by Tristano Martinelli, the actor of the commedia dell'arte, who at the end of the sixteenth century created in France the masked character of Harlequin.

In fact, the primordial Harlequin did not perform leaps and graceful acrobatics in the manner of Goldoni's fools. On the contrary he jumped around like a monkey, making aggressive grunts.

In one of the first scenarios, Harlequin defecated in the middle of the stage, and then went into the audience shamelessly groping all the women, and even a priest that he mistook for a woman because of his robes.

The masks of the company that acted with him on the stage: Pantalone, Brighella, Smeraldina, etc., express sympathy and tenderness for this diabolical Zanni, as did the audience at court, including the king and queen, who greeted him with much laughter and applause the scurrilous and surreal antics of Arlek, Arlequin, Arlecchino (Harlequin). But we see that little by little the "wild" Zanni was domesticated, and transformed into a being that was more human, almost civilized, with his own original ideas.

At this point Harlequin was no longer interesting, or funny . . . to the contrary, he was boring. In fact, in the end, when he was presented as a well-mannered man, asking for food . . . we see that he was kicked around by everyone and thrown off the stage.

This is a theme that could make a good play for our times!

Returning to "The Birth of the Peasant"—it is also relevant to certain entrepreneurs that we find in our times!

Traveling around Italy, we are continually confronted with events that can only be called grotesque. For example, once we arrived in Verona for a show, and found ourselves in that theatre completely covered in flags and banners that hundreds of young people had tacked onto every wall. The writings denounced the conditions they had to endure in the factory. They were all on strike to protest the rules that the owner of the textile factory had imposed on them in regards to the bodily needs of the workers.

That is, when one felt the urge to go: "Excuse me, may I?" "No . . . and no!" They all had to go to the toilet at 11:25 A.M.—DRIIIIN—and pee-pee. And if they didn't have to go at that time, too bad. The next chance was at 5:10 P.M. They had threatened to occupy the factory to gain the right to relieve themselves on a free schedule.

That night, together with the young people on strike and the audience, we wrote a song that we later performed in the play *We Think and We Sing!* If you allow me, I will perform it for you: "Don't Get Angry, Mister Boss":

Don't get angry, Mister Boss,
If I have to go to the toilet.

You went the day before yesterday
Do you have to go every day?
Do you want to ruin me
And slow down the assembly line?

Mister Boss, I promise
That starting tomorrow I won't go.

I'll only eat soups,
And pee.
I'll do it here!

Go on, but hurry. Three minutes.
Like it says in the contract:
No smoking in the toilet,
No reading *Unity*,
Because the periscope will see you.

Six seconds to get there
Six seconds to get undressed
Three seconds for sitting down
The foreman comes to get you
Nothing to do but hurry.
Three seconds for standing up
Two seconds for getting dressed
If you're lucky you can wash
And run right back to work
To work
To work.

THE RITE OF THE GOATS
AND MAMMUTHONES

A slide of a painting is projected on a backdrop.

GIULLARE: Look, this is a depiction of a "buffonata," that is to say a kind of preparation for grotesquely ironic spectacles that drew the personal participation of the people in the district or neighborhood, all dressed up and disguised. Here you see them. *(Points to people in the projected image)* This one went all the way to the point of disguising himself as one of the mammuthones.

What are the "mammuthones"?

They are ancient masks—half goat, half devil. Still today in Sardegna, the peasants and shepherds, during the festivals of the spring and summer solstices, wear masks of different animals (rams, goats and bulls), and cover themselves with all kinds of animal pelts, and put on lots of cowbells. They leap through the streets like this, terrorizing women and children who run away screaming. The mammuthones put on masks, as you can see in this slide, that depict the faces of bestial devils. Look, this is a giullare, this is the character called "Jolly," the fool—an allegory of unsanctioned thoughts. And this is another devil. *(Points)* Still another one. *(Points again)*

Here is another sequence. *(A second slide depicting a grotesque procession is projected)* Devils, witches and an ornamental monk passing by. Note another detail: they all have instruments for making noise, because the game of making a racket, a hubbub, was essential in these festivals. *(Pointing to a character in the grotesque procession)* This one even has in his hand a "ciccine" from Napoli, constructed from a drum that has a pole stuck inside that he moves in a way sufficient to produce mangled groans and trumpeting.

Here is another buffoon with his leg up in the air, who doesn't need any instruments. He is a self-producing noisemaker, generating trumpets and groans all on his own, organically. *(Pointing to another group of characters)* These others produce different sounds.

During the buffoonery the masked characters all gathered together in the piazza to organize a kind of fake (but realistic) procession of the nobility, the landowners, including merchants, emperors, usurers, bankers, who in the Middle Ages were part of the same class (of course this was only in the Middle Ages)—a spectacle that contained pointed accusations of exploitation and deceit. Also making conspicuous appearances were the figures of bishops and cardinals. (I never understood why, in ancient times, holy men of the church were always lumped together with blatant hypocrites and perpetrators of simony. How times have changed!)

The triumphant moment of the grotesque tribunal came at the finale—a kind of hell—in which all the upper-class characters fell head over heels into giant pots of boiling oil (fake, of course).

In the end, the assemblage of lower-class characters— women and men all in masks—entered the church, preceded by mimes, acrobats and clowns.

The Church in the Middle Ages respected the original meaning of "ecclesiam," which was a place of assemblage. Often present at the grotesque rite was the bishop in person, who stood at the transept waiting for the protagonists of the buffonata. The bishop took off all his vestments and offered them to the leader of the giullari, who climbed up onto the pulpit and gave the beginning of a homily, a sermon (on the same theme of the sermon normally presented by the bishop), performing it in parody.

When the giullare was very gifted, he succeeded in eliciting ovations from the audience of the faithful, who split their sides laughing. The public picked up all the ironic references and allusions of the satire, which was performed in a language so powerful that it seemed to be bestowed and blessed by the creator in person.

It is said that in Brescia, in the time of the "Comuni" [Italian city-states], there was a bishop known as Ilario, who was subjected to such ferocious ridicule and irony during the carnivalesque oration of the giullare that he couldn't gather the strength to climb back up onto the pulpit to deliver his own sermons, because as soon as he would begin to preach, his audience burst out into wild laughter, which ended with them rolling in the aisles weeping tears of joy that were filled with the authentic mysticism of side-splitting laughter.

There are also stories of another bishop, His Eminence of Ferrara, who tried to avoid the difficulty of reclaiming his credibility after each satirical assault by refusing to consign his robes to the king of the carnival. And he also tried to stop the crowd of maskers from invading the cathedral during the four days of the "Ghignata." The enraged populace hounded the bishop out of the city.

Moving along to the next slide *(Slide is projected)*, we find the depiction of another sacred representation, this time one that is both dramatic and grotesque at the same time. It is a performance that took place in Flanders around 1360—the date is inscribed on the engraving. You can see here is a woman with a lamb in her arms. I point it out to you because it alludes to the text of the peasant passion play: "The Massacre of the Innocents."

Let's move on. *(The next slide is projected)* Here is another important image. We are in Anversa in 1465, the exact year of the first edict of Toledo. The Toledo edict was the one that definitively forbade the people from performing the comic mystery plays. And you can understand from this image the reason for this censorship. You can see that there is an actor interpreting the role of Jesus Christ, and here are two thugs. Here is a thief, played by another actor, and the people below them are responding to the line spoken by the thief.

And what does the thief propose? He shouts: "Who do you want on the cross? Jesus Christ or Barabbas?"

And the crowd below them responds, shouting: "Jean Gloughert!" who was the mayor of the city.

So you can see why that powerful man was not very fond of the giullari.

A performance of this type, actually one that was considerably more violent, is depicted in the next slide. *(The next slide)* It's Paris. We are in the old "Place du Louvre," still around the same period. We discover in this little theatre an actor, who is performing the role of Jesus Christ, and other actors. Next to him we see Pontius Pilate with the basin ready. He is about to dip his fingers into it, and in front of him are two bishops . . . and you can see that they are two Catholic bishops. Shouldn't they be wearing the ritual clothing of Jews, with completely different decorative details, starting with the classic headgear of the rabbis of Israel? Instead, the crude organizers of the play, pretending to know nothing about the costumes of the period, have inserted into the action two bishops performing Roman Catholic apostolic rites. And believe me, it was not a mere lapsus, or a simple anachronistic error.

(Another slide) Here is a giullare who is acting out an allegory from the Bible. It is a representation of the famous drinking bout of King David. The Bible tells us that one day David drank in abundance. During this drinking bout he got a little carried away, ostentatiously singing and dancing to the applause of the others who were drunk like him, but scandalizing those who were sober. In his wine-induced euphoria, he was transformed into a true giullare, even making fun of his father, not only his earthly father but the one in heaven as well, and he took aim at his own subjects as well, particularly those who were "poor and indentured." The giullare, dressed in sumptuous robes that recalled those of the king, performed in the piazza reciting: "And you . . . down there . . . poor and underfed," he shouted, "you and you and you and you

and also your women—you all work for me and for those who command you like I do and if you complain I'll smash you to hell, because it is true that I have been elected . . . and also anointed by God! *By God!* So you will put up with all the nonsense they feed you, and believe that the land was granted to your masters by God himself. No, you piss-heads, they gobbled up the land because they were quicker than you and then they tethered you to it so that you could work the land for the pittance you deserve!"

Now you understand the reason why giullari were so often chased away from the cities, and also from the countryside.

There was one, a certain Hans Holden. *(Pointing to the next slide)* There he is . . . a famous German giullare, superb in his comic portrayal of the drunken David, who dared to present the piece in the piazza ignoring the edict that forbade the performance. He ended up burnt at the stake.

In the Middle Ages there was a custom that consisted of a particular kind of public "beating" to announce sacred spectacles. Still today, in Puglia, during the festival of the patron saint of the city, Saint Nicolas of Bari—a famous black bishop who came from the east—they enact these processions.

Today this festival is reduced to a generic parade in which floats are carried depicting painted scenes, whose significance is no longer understood by the faithful. In ancient times these paintings illustrated the various scenes that would be performed for the public later in the evening. Behind them were the "battuti," also known as the "flagellants," who went around whipping the bejesus out of themselves . . . it wasn't for nothing that they called it a sacred spectacle!

The same rite is still performed today in the procession of Good Friday in Veneto. They sing, accompanied by lots of flagellation, more or less like this:

("Chant of the Flagellants":)

Ohioihioh—beat, beat yourselves!
Ehiaiehieh!
Companions, line yourselves up,
Beat yourselves hard and willfully,
Do not lament the blows—beat yourselves!
Have no fear of being naked,
Have no fear of the whips that wound you,
Ripping and stripping your flesh.

Ohioohioh—beat, beat yourselves!
Ehiaiehieh!
Whoever wants to save themselves,
Should beat themselves with the whip,
Landing shocking lashes with the whip,
Do not pretend to deliver the blows—beat yourselves!
Like the all-powerful Lord
Was truly beaten.

Ohiohioh—beat, beat yourselves!
Ehiaiaehieh!
If you want to do penance
And reduce the huge sentence
That is about to be passed down on you
That no one can escape—beat yourselves!
That will fall on our backs.

Ohi—let us beat ourselves painfully!
Ehiaiehieh!
To purify ourselves of sin.
Jesus Christ was beaten,
He was nailed on the cross,
And they spit on his face—beat yourselves!
And he was given vinegar to drink,
And Saint Peter was not there.

Ohioihioh—beat, beat yourselves!
Ehiaiehieh!
And you masters of usury,
You of ill fortune,

You who have spit on Christ,
Enriching yourselves with ill-gotten wealth—beat
yourselves!
You who have pressed like grapes
The money of those who sweat for it.
Ohioihioh—beat, beat yourselves!
Ehiaiehieh!

THE MASSACRE OF
THE INNOCENTS

A few years ago at the abbey of Chiaravalle near Milan there was an extraordinary exhibition of theatrical machinery. It consisted of polychrome wooden statues with moving body parts that were articulated like puppets or dolls. The movements were controlled through a series of hooks and levers that were manipulated by a puppeteer positioned behind a special backdrop, or in the case of the large statues, hidden inside the back of the sculpture, which was not fully rounded, but completed only on the front half. Among them was a fabulous "Madonna and Child" from 1100, in which both characters moved arms, torsos, elbows and even the eyes, also playing the trick of disequilibrium devised by Flemish puppeteers. For example, there was an equalizer in the forearm and an articulated joint inside the wrist, connected to a hinge, so that the tiniest movement would initiate a rotation of the hand over the wrist before it regained a stabilized equilibrium. The same thing occurred for each of the other body parts, so that every movement produced gestures of extraordinary grace—it gave the impression of something alive.

　　In the cathedral of San Zeno in Verona, one can still admire a Christ sitting on the back of an ass. The ass has wheels inserted in his hooves that allow the rider and his steed to be dragged along in a procession representing the famous and triumphant arrival in Jerusalem.

Using the same principle, another famous piece was constructed, the Christ of Aquileia. In this theatrical sculpture the numerous articulated joints are not visible because the body is completely covered in draped robes.

Why did the organizers of medieval mystery plays choose to bring the saints onto the stage in the form of rolling sculptures? Perhaps they feared that the use of actors would damage the sacred nature of the divine characters and thus risk committing an act of blasphemy? Yes, this was one of the worries. But the real reason they preferred to employ moving statues for the role of Christ, the Virgin and the others was determined by the difficulty of the task taken on by the actor/storyteller in the presentation of the drama, lending his voice and gestures to the characters, commenting, and often addressing the audience in provocative tones, and working them up into an extraordinary emotional state.

The moving sculptures almost came to be viewed as stage assistants. The storyteller moved among the indicated characters like a stage manager, succeeding in this way to underscore more clearly the passion of the Son of God and, almost in counterpoint, the drama of the human condition—desperation, hunger, pain.

I have brought up this theme of theatrical machines, because the piece that Franca will now perform anticipates their use: the entrance on the stage of a rolling statue that represents the Madonna with her baby in her arms. With her in the dramatic action we have a crazy woman who holds in her arms, wrapped in a shawl, a lamb.

Now you see why, a little while ago, I pointed out to you that Flemish slide, in which one could see a woman with a lamb in her arms.[2] It is taken from the same dramatic situation that we will present to you in a few moments: a mother, whose baby has been killed during the massacre of the innocents, has been driven mad by grief. The woman has lost her sense of reason, and has taken a lamb from a sheep pen, holding it in her arms and going around telling everyone that it is her son who escaped the massacre. The allegory is clear: the lamb is the "Agnus Dei," the Son of God, so that this woman is also the Virgin.

36   2. See "The Rite of the Goats and Mammuthones."

This double role of the madwoman/Madonna is quite old; it even surfaced during the time of the Greeks. The mother, out of her mind, is allowed to say things that an actress playing the role of the Madonna would not be permitted to even suggest.

And so, with the excuse of madness, the crazy woman lets loose insults against the Heavenly Creator. She says in a loud voice: "You should have kept your son close to you, if he was going to cost us so much suffering, so much pain!" And she continues at length along those lines.

It is certainly the strongest curse ever heard in a sacred performance.

Through this scenic device the faithful of certain communities (the ideas of some of the Cathar sects come to mind) harshly criticized the Heavenly Father for having favored some social classes to the complete detriment of the great majority of men, who were trapped into intolerable conditions of frustration, injustice and desperate poverty.

In contrast, Jesus Christ was not only well accepted, but also loved and cheered as a liberator. And the God who makes mankind and comes onto the Earth to give hope again, offers them springtime and, above all, dignity. The discussion of dignity is, in these stories of the people, continually raised again and again, almost like a recurring motif, with incredible insistence.

Now we are going to perform "The Massacre of the Innocents." I should point out one detail in particular: the language. The language, the dialect, actually the vernacular, spoken on the plains of the Po river from the thirteenth to fifteenth centuries. The actor or actress who performed these sacred or profane pieces traveled on foot from town to town, following in the path of various festivals and religious feasts. And knowing that the spoken vernacular of a vast region like Padania could never be homogeneous, the giullari were forced to adapt their texts in order to make themselves understood, inserting local terms to make their speeches more accessible. But this approach was often insufficient, so the itinerant actors began to invent a language that could be understood all over, a kind of lingua franca, composed of altered expressions taken from various dialects and diverse idioms: Provençal, Catalan and even Latin. But the cornerstone of this theatrical language was rooted in onomatopoeia. That is to say, they chose expressions whose sounds and rhythms already alluded clearly to a specific concept or situation.

On the topic of linguistic devices, I'll tell you an anecdote whose protagonist is a young girl, a virgin, who finds herself in the arms of a man with whom she is madly in love. The piece is from the fourteenth century and is recounted by a giullare from Bologna, who tells how the young girl decides to make love with the man she loves, but when the moment comes for their passionate embrace, the girl is blocked, suddenly afraid, fearing the violence of the embrace. She puts out her arms, distancing the man from her, and says in a trembling voice: "Please, don't touch me, because I'm just a little girl, I'm a maiden, I'm a baby doll, I'm a sweet young thing, I'm a kid."

In short, she repeated, without taking a breath, in five different idioms: "I'm a child, I'm a child, I'm a child, I'm a child." This device is called iteration, but it doesn't just have the advantage of making oneself understood more clearly, it also produces the almost lyrical effect of capturing the anxiety of the dramatic situation.

A while ago we discussed the use of the flagellants in sacred performances. Often these singers, who whipped themselves in obsessive rhythms, were given the task of introducing the various tragic and comic scenes with short litanies that they presented during the pauses between scenes in the drama. Above all, the timbered shouts of their drums closed each tragic sequence and commented on it. A specific example is this fragment that introduces "The Massacre of the Innocents," musically similar to that which you have already heard [in "The Rite of the Goats . . .]. The lashes are whipped violently but each flagellant keeps hidden in his fist a sponge, soaked in a red-colored broth. At the moment of the whipping, pretending to dry themselves, they spray the vermillion liquid onto their backs. Some penitents, when they first enter the fraternity of the flagellants, whip themselves with real lashes, in bursts of unimaginable violence—their screams of pain are authentic and so is the spilling of their blood. Under their hooded robes, the veteran flagellants split their sides laughing.

CHORUS OF FLAGELLANTS:
    Ohioihi—beat, beat yourselves!
    Ehiaiehieh!

With pain and lamentation
For the massacre of the innocents,
A thousand innocent little children,
They butchered them like baby goats,
From their dazed mothers
King Herod has torn them away.
Ohioihi—beat, beat yourselves!
Ehaiehieh!
Ahaiaiheih!
(In extreme falsetto) Ahiaeeeee!

(On the stage we find two Soldiers and a Mother. The Soldiers are about to kill the woman's son.)

FIRST MOTHER: Murderer . . . pig . . . don't touch my baby.
FIRST SOLDIER: Let it go . . . drop the baby or I'll cut off your hands . . . I'll give you a kick in the stomach . . . let go!
FIRST MOTHER *(Desperate)*: Noooo! Kill me instead.

(The First Soldier succeeds in tearing the child out of his Mother's arms and killing him; a horrific scream from the Mother.)

Ahaaaa. Ahaaa . . . you killed him, you slaughtered him.

(The traumatized Mother leaves the stage, crying desperately, holding the butchered child close to her chest.
Another Mother enters, holding in her arms a baby that is completely wrapped in a shawl.)

SECOND SOLDIER: Oh, look, there's another one . . . Stop where you are, woman . . . or I'll stab the both of you . . . you and your baby!
SECOND MOTHER: Go ahead and stab us, because that's what I prefer . . .
SECOND SOLDIER: Don't play the fool . . . you're still young and you have time to have another dozen babies . . . just give me this one . . . be a good girl. *(Tries to pull the baby away from her)*

SECOND MOTHER: No . . . take your paws off me! *(Bites his hand)*
SECOND SOLDIER: Ahia—you want to bite, eh . . . then take this! *(Gives her a violent slap)* and let go of this bundle!
SECOND MOTHER *(Desperately defending her baby)*: Have pity, please . . . don't kill him . . . I'll give you everything I have . . .

(The Second Soldier manages to strip the bundle from the Mother's arms. In the struggle, the shawl falls to the ground and the Second Soldier finds himself with a baby lamb in his arms.)

SECOND SOLDIER: Hey, what's this? A sheep . . . a baby lamb?!
SECOND MOTHER: Oh yes, it's not a baby, it's a sheep . . . I never had a baby . . . I'm not able to, I can't. *(Imploring)* Oh, please, Soldier, don't kill my baby lamb . . . because it's not Easter yet . . . and you'd be committing a big sin if you killed it!
SECOND SOLDIER: Come on, lady! Do you take me for a retard . . . or maybe you're crazy.
SECOND MOTHER: Me, crazy? No I'm not crazy!
FIRST SOLDIER: Let's go, leave the lamb . . .

(The Second Soldier gives the lamb back to the Mother. She leaves.)

She's out of her mind with grief because we killed her son.

(The Second Soldier puts his hand over his stomach and bends over.)

What's wrong with you? Get moving, we still have a whole lot more of them to cut up.
SECOND SOLDIER: Wait . . . I'm going to throw up . . .
FIRST SOLDIER: Some soldier you are! You eat like a cow: onions, salted mutton and then . . . Come here to the corner, there's a tavern . . . I'll get you a nice big swig of grappa.
SECOND SOLDIER: No, it's not about eating! It's about this butchery, this slaughtering of babies, it's what we're doing that turns my stomach.

40

FIRST SOLDIER: If you knew you were so sensitive, you shouldn't have taken up soldiering.

SECOND SOLDIER: I became a soldier to kill grown-up enemies.

FIRST SOLDIER: And maybe to knock some woman down into the straw . . . eh?

SECOND SOLDIER: Well, if it happened—but only enemy women!

FIRST SOLDIER: And slaughter some livestock—

SECOND SOLDIER: —of the enemy!

FIRST SOLDIER: Burn down some houses . . . kill a few old folks . . . some roosters . . . and babies—only enemy babies!

SECOND SOLDIER: Yes, babies too . . . but in battle! There's no dishonor in war: the trumpets are blowing, the drums are rolling and the battle songs and the beautiful words of the commanders urging you on.

FIRST SOLDIER: Oh, but for this butchery also, you have the beautiful words of the commanders!

SECOND SOLDIER: But here the ones we're killing are innocent!

FIRST SOLDIER: And why isn't everyone in war innocent? What have they done to you? Did they offend your blood, those poor bastards that you stab and kill to the sound of the trumpets?

(A mannequin of the Madonna and her child appears in the background.)

Either I'm going blind or that's the Virgin Mary and the baby that we're looking for! Let's get them, before they escape . . . get going . . . we can get the reward . . . it's huge!

SECOND SOLDIER: I don't want that lousy, stinking reward!

FIRST SOLDIER: Fine, then I'll take it myself!

SECOND SOLDIER: No, you're not going to take it either. *(Blocks his path)*

FIRST SOLDIER: Hey, have you gone mad? Let me by. We have orders to kill the son of the Virgin.

SECOND SOLDIER: I shit on those orders! Don't take a step or I'll crush you!

FIRST SOLDIER: Poor bastard . . . you haven't understood yet that if this baby stays alive, he'll become the king of Galilee in Herod's place . . . that's what the prophecy said.

SECOND SOLDIER: I shit on Herod and the prophecy too!

FIRST SOLDIER: You need to relieve yourself, and not just your stomach . . . so, go out in a field somewhere and let me by . . . because I don't want to lose the reward!

SECOND SOLDIER: No, I've had enough of seeing babies butchered!

FIRST SOLDIER: Then it's too bad for you!

(The First Soldier stabs him with his sword.)

SECOND SOLDIER *(Holding his hand over his stomach)*: Ahia— you screwed me . . . you miserable wretch . . . you cut my guts open.

FIRST SOLDIER: I'm sorry . . . you were being a ball-buster . . . I didn't mean to . . .

SECOND SOLDIER: I'm pissing blood all over . . . Oh, Mamma . . . Mamma . . . where are you, Mamma . . . It's getting dark . . . I'm cold, Mamma . . . Mamma . . .

(The Second Soldier falls to the ground, dead.)

FIRST SOLDIER: I didn't kill him, I didn't . . . that one was a cadaver from the moment he started to feel pity: "A soldier who feels a mercy attack, might just as well be flat on his back." That's what the proverb says. And meanwhile he made me lose the chance to grab the Virgin and her baby!

(While the First Soldier drags away the body of his companion, the mannequin representing the Madonna is slid fully onto the stage. Entering by her side is the crazy Mother with the lamb in her arms, still wrapped in the shawl. The Chorus of Flagellants, singing softly, reprises its lament:)

CHORUS OF FLAGELLANTS:
Ohioihi—beat, beat yourselves!
Ehiaiehieh!
With pain and lamentation

For the massacre of the innocents,
Thousands of innocent little children,
They butchered them like baby goats,
From their dazed mothers
King Herod has torn them away.
Ohiohihi—beat, beat yourselves
Ehiaiehieh!

SECOND MOTHER *(Turning to the mannequin of the Madonna)*:
Don't run away, Madonna. Don't try to escape, don't be afraid, because I'm not a soldier. I'm a woman . . . a mother like you with my baby. You can hide here safely because the soldiers have gone away. Don't be afraid . . . the massacre is over, the butchery is over. Don't cry, don't tremble. Sit down, poor woman, who has been forced to run so far! Let me see your baby . . . Oh, he's so pretty and colorful! Beautiful, beautiful . . . he's so happy. Oh what an adorable face he has! He'll have good times ahead! How old is he? He looks about the same age as mine. What's his name? Jesus? That's a pretty name! *(To the baby)* Jesus! Beautiful, beautiful . . . Jesuino. He's laughing . . . he's already got two teeth! Oh, how cute! Mine doesn't have teeth yet, he's been a little sick this month, but now he's doing better. He's here sleeping like a little angel. *(Calls to him)* Marco? *(To the Madonna)* His name is Marco. He's a heavy sleeper. *(To her son)* Oh, darling, you're so beautiful! You are a beauty, you little Marcolino! *(To the Madonna)* It's a fact that we mothers have a built-in instinct, so that even if our baby has a few defects . . . no, no you can't even tell. I love this little beast so much, that if they ever took him away from me I'd go mad! If I think of the pain . . . of the fear that came over me this morning when I woke up. I heard shouting . . . I went to the cradle and it was empty . . . full of blood and my little son wasn't there anymore . . . And I heard soldiers shouting outside in the street. I ran. There were mothers crying desperately . . . and butchered babies! "They killed him! They killed my baby!" I started shouting in a daze: "They killed him!"

Luckily it wasn't true . . . it was just a dream . . . but I didn't know it. Even as I was slowly waking up I still had the impression that I was dreaming, and I was so desperate I seemed like a crazy woman, I went out into the court-yard and started cursing the Lord: "Pitiless and awful God," I shouted, "You ordered this murdering . . . You wanted this sacrifice in exchange for sending down your son: a thousand babies butchered for your one! A river of blood for a tiny cupful. Better you should have kept him close to you, this son, if he was going to cost us poor wretches such a sacrifice . . . Oh, even you will find out in the end what it means to be crushed by grief on the day your son dies on the cross! You will also come to under-stand in the end what a wretched and awful punishment you have imposed on mankind throughout eternity! Father, you are not kind, you . . . are not a father! Because no father on earth would have ever had the heart to impose such a thing on his son, for how horrid it must be to be crucified."

I was mistaken, Madonna . . . do you understand me? . . . I cursed because I didn't understand . . . I was out of my mind . . . Suddenly, I turned my eyes and inside the sheep pen, in the middle of the sheep, I discovered my baby cry-ing! He called out: "Baaaaa, baaaaaa . . ." Like a little lamb . . . it was my son! I recognized him right away. I ran to the sheep pen . . . What was my baby doing in there with the sheep? There he was on all fours. I took him in my arms . . . I squeezed him . . . I kissed him . . . and I started to cry for joy: "Please forgive me most merciful Lord for those ugly words I shouted without thinking. It was the devil . . . it was the devil who is always nearby . . . whis-pering in my ear . . . he was the one who made me say it! You are so kind, Lord, to have saved my son! And you did it in a way that made everyone mistake him for a real baby lamb. And even the soldiers didn't realize it, and they let me go free!"

I'd better be careful though. Easter is coming soon, and that's when they start killing little lambs just like they were killing babies today. The butchers will come looking for him. But I'll put a bonnet on his head and wrap him all up in rags, so that he'll be mistaken for a baby. But then I'll be careful not to let anyone recognize that he is a baby . . . I'll take him out to pastures and teach him to eat grass so that it will seem to everyone that he is a sheep . . . because it will be easier for my son to live as a sheep than as a man in this miserable world!

(She changes tone) Oh, yes he's woken up . . . he's laughing! Look, Madonna, how beautiful he is, like a little blossom ready to be picked, my little Marcolino . . .

(The Mother pulls down the shawl and shows the Madonna the little lamb that she is holding in her arms. The statue of the Virgin responds with a start and leans its head toward its shoulder.)

Oh, Madonna, are you all right? What's happening to you? Why are you trembling? Is it because you are afraid, Madonna? No one's there . . . the soldiers have gone away . . . the sun is covered by clouds . . . it's going to rain and all the blood on the walls and the ground will be washed away, Mary! You're smiling at me, Madonna . . . you're smiling at me. Oh, your cute little baby is smiling, too. Look . . . how pretty! Jesuino? Do you want to sleep? Mine is sleepy, too. Let's sing them a lullaby together, Mary. You sing to yours and I'll sing to mine . . . we'll lullaby them both together . . . and put them to sleep. Do you want to sing, Madonna? (Cradling the baby, she sings:)

Lullaby, lullaby,
You're Mamma's pretty baby.
The Madonna cradles you
While the angels sing,
Saint Joseph is asleep on his feet,
Baby Jesus laughs,
And Herod curses
A thousand babies fly to heaven
Lullaby, lullaby
Lullaby, lullaby . . .

(While the lights slowly fade, the voice of the Second Mother is drowned out by the song of the Chorus of Flagellants:)

CHORUS OF FLAGELLANTS:
>Ohioihi—beat, beat yourselves!
>Ehiaiehieh!
>With pain and lamentation
>For the massacre of the innocents,
>A thousand innocent little children,
>They butchered them like baby lambs,
>From their dazed mothers
>King Herod tore them away.
>Ohioihi—beat, beat yourselves!
>Ehiaiehieh!
>And thank the Lord,
>Most merciful,
>For having driven the desperate out of their minds
>So they don't have to endure the pain!
>Ohioihi—beat, beat yourselves!
>Ehiaiehieh!

THE FIRST MIRACLE
OF THE CHILD JESUS

PROLOGUE

The following monologue is entitled "The First Miracle of the Child Jesus" and it is taken from the Apocryphal Gospels. It is known that for the original Christians "apocryphal" did not mean false, heretical or blasphemous, but referred simply to things that were not included in the official Gospels. Some of these writings were kept hidden so that they would be seen only by the initiated.

In the third and fourth centuries there were known to be dozens of Gospels that today we find published in a great number of editions. The most complete of those editions is the one edited by Giulio Einaudi.

Every Christian community had its Gospels, which evolved and were performed.

The selection of the Gospels that were acceptable lasted many centuries. Many episodes concerning the life of Jesus were crossed off the official list because they represented situations and moral principles that conflicted with the writings of the four evangelists: Matthew, Mark, Luke and John.

The miracle of the child Jesus belongs to a group of Gospels that was discarded. In the collections of writings that were not officially recognized are found stories linked to ancient Greek myths, in which we meet Christ, who, like Orpheus, plays the flute and charms the animals around him with his music. Other stores are linked to the Orient with dragons and galloping steeds that Christ rides with agility, practically transforming himself into a centaur. In short, because their narratives did not conform to the canonical imagery, a great number of Gospels determined to be apocryphal were put aside, but often it was decided that they should be destroyed.

In the sixth and seventh centuries, in a famous council, an incredible debate erupted between various bishops from diverse communities. Each one battled for the acceptance and recognition of his own vision of the life of Christ, and above all for their own particular interpretation of the Word as expressed by the Messiah. As had already happened in the Council of Nicea in 325, the holy delegates insulted one another, attacked one another, sometimes provoking physical fights. In the end many texts ended up torn to pieces on the ground. Many of the delegates were wounded and some of them might even have died. Evidence of these terrible battles can be found in the current shape of the bishop's pastoral staff, which was bent as a result of all the blows and counterpunches, which, little by little, twisted it at the top. Even the hat worn by bishops and cardinals—you know the split down the middle? It is a mark that still attests to the blows that they delivered to one another.

This truly poetic episode about the childhood of Christ that we are presenting to you was regularly read and commented on in the sixth century in the churches of the Orient. And even today it is recited and sung in the sacred festivals that take place in the towns of Irpinia and Salento.

The so-called official version of the New Testament tells the story of the birth of the Savior with the Nativity scene, the gifts of the Magi, the flight to Egypt, the presentation at the temple, and the dialogue between young Jesus and the wise men of the synagogue. Then, after that, Jesus disappears, and we know nothing else about his childhood. We see him again as an adult by the Jordan River at the moment he asks John to baptize him.

In the Apocryphal Gospels, this void in the story is filled with a number of notable episodes about the childhood of Jesus, of which this first miracle, we can guess, might have been considered a genuine masterpiece of allegorical fantasy.

The sacred family, fleeing to Egypt with their donkey, goes towards the sea and they get as far as Jaffa. Jaffa is the city of grapefruits. At the mention of this city's name the audience always explodes into hearty laughter, a kind of snickering that is rooted in a big mistake. Some of the audience believes, erroneously, that I am referring to the stamp that we find today on the grapefruits that are produced in that region; I'm talking about the "J" stamped on the fruit . . . that it might just as well stand for Jesus.

For pity's sake . . . that is not the miracle of the child Jesus. His first miracle had a completely different power and sense of wonder. The little boy arrived in Jaffa with his family, and in that land they were strangers, outsiders, and impoverished. They immediately started looking for a place to live and found a miserable hovel . . . so shabby that it made their manger in Bethlehem seem like a palace in comparison. Joseph, who was a carpenter, went looking for work, but couldn't find any. He couldn't find a nail to hammer. The Madonna, to earn a little money, was forced to go out and wash laundry for other families. Little Jesus found himself abandoned in the street all day. He sees children playing. He watches the games of the kids in the neighborhood and he wants to find a way to join in, be included, but instead he is chased away. He is an outsider. He speaks another dialect, almost another language.

It is well known, and we can verify it daily in the housing projects of our suburbs, that wherever racism exists, children are more racist than adults, and so the child Jesus, humiliated, in order to be accepted into the group, performs his astounding little miracle, as a child would perform a miracle, and achieves an extraordinary success: everyone hugs him and elects him leader of the games. —Laughter, shouts of enthusiasm, the mothers applauding from the windows! But then look who enters the scene, riding on the back of a small pony with golden saddling, the son of the richest man in the city, accompanied by two henchmen. The child of the rich man demands to participate in the new game, but the little ragamuffins don't let him. The offspring of the master, red with rage, is offended and destroys all the children's toys.

The reaction of the child Jesus is astonishing . . . one might say he had all the saints spinning in their graves. One never sees Jesus so enraged. Never as an adult does he react so violently—not even when he is angry with the merchants for defiling the sanctity of the temple.

The rhythm and scenic synthesis that we find in this episode, as is the case in other Apocryphal Gospels, is truly extraordinary.

I would even venture to say that it has a surprising modernity. It is as if we find ourselves in the hands of a screenwriter for a master of contemporary avant-garde cinema. And in a little while I'm sure that, after listening to the startling immediacy of this piece about the first miracle, you will agree with me.

In performing this story, I am using a language that combines many northern dialects, primarily Venetian.

———

GIULLARE: Suddenly in the star-studded night sky, glistening with light, there appeared a tremendously large star . . . with a huge wagging tail that struck the stars around it like a whip, making them shout, "Who the hell is that?"

It was the comet! It came from the east and following close behind it were the three Magi.

One was old, very sullen, muttering curses on a black horse . . . (Pay attention to the allegory!) And as he rode this black horse he pushed against the stirrups to lift up his buttocks, because it was covered with boils and blisters right there on his butt . . . and every bump pounded his ass into the saddle and made him shout and curse like God betrayed!

Close to him was a blond Wise Man, young and pale, with a full head of curly golden hair . . . who rode a white horse . . . (Pay attention to the allegory!) with shining eyes and a laughing mouth . . . On his back was a large cloak of red and silver.

The last in line was a black Magus on a gray camel . . . (Keep paying attention to the allegory!) A black man, very black, with dark pupils centered in the whites of his eyes, a white so white that when he laughed, the gray camel beneath him seemed more clear and white than the white horse of the blond Magus.

These shaman kings went moving along, as the black one on his camel sang:

Oh it's swell, it's swell, it's swell
To be riding a camel.
With our gems, with our gems,

We're on our way to Bethlehem.
In Bethlehem we'll go to the manger
Where Madonna's family's safe from danger
And the baby will be crying
While Saint Joseph stands there sighing
And the angels all are flying
Oh it's swell, it's swell, it's swell
To be riding a camel!

"That's enough," shouted the old king Magus. "You've been singing this camel jingle for three days and three nights! We all know how swell it is to ride a camel, but now shut up about it already!"

(In the singing rhythm of the nursery rhyme:)

Oh no, I cannot stop,
'Cause my camel loves bebop
I've got to keep on singing,
That's what keeps my camel swinging,
If I lose the music's beat
Then my camel falls asleep
And he'll fall right off his feet
And crush me underneath
Then I won't get to Bethlehem
To give the holy kid the gems
No, I've got to get there to the manger
Where Madonna's family's safe from danger
And the baby will be crying
While Saint Joseph stands there sighing
And the angels all are flying
Oh it's swell, it's swell, it's swell
To be riding a camel!

"That's enough! I'm going to eat you alive! I'll peel off all the black on the outside and eat up all the white on the inside! Stop singing!"

The black king Magus continued his rhyming:

Oh, no, I've got to keep on singing.
The rhythm keeps my camel swinging
Because a camel's not like a horse
That simply gallops on its course
A camel trots instead
One leg back, one leg ahead.
This camel runs at quite a clip
Without a rhythm it'll trip
Fall right off its feet
And crush me underneath
Then I'll never get these gems
To the kid in Bethlehem
Where Madonna found a manger
To keep her family out of danger
And the baby will be crying
While Saint Joseph stands there crying
And the angels all are flying . . .

"I'm going to devour you!!!" *(Almost lifting his head to the Heavenly Father)* "I don't understand why they had to bring this black man with all the other colored Magi kings that are around! Why him? . . ." *(As if remembering the prophecy)* "Ah, we have to be 'cosmopolitan'! Well this black man is a very good person, but he can't keep on singing like that! . . . Sometimes he frightens me! Sometimes nature calls . . ." *(He points to his rear end)* ". . . With the boils that are popping up all over down there . . . I'm a Magus, but when you have to go, you have to go! I get off my horse, go off into the dark of the night . . . get ready to pull down my trousers . . . when all of a sudden, right in front of me, I see two beastly eyes . . . with beastly teeth . . . Dammit, it's a lion! . . . And I shit in my pants! But it was just him, taking a shit in front of me . . . and laughing. Shitting and laughing . . . and not singing! It was the first time he stopped singing! Couldn't he at least have sung: 'Oh it's swell, it's swell, it's swell/To take a shit without a camel.' Then I would have known who it was!

"He scared the shit out of me . . . So between all the boils on my butt and him, I'm going to be in such a state of rage when I get to Bethlehem that I'll strangle the baby in his cradle."

At that moment the big star in the sky stopped moving and everyone asked, "What's happening?"

And the black Magus sang:

It just stopped to catch its breath!
Oh it's swell, it's swell, it's swell
To be going to Bethlehem . . .

(To the black Magus bouncing on his camel) "Enooooough!"

The old Magus jumped onto his black horse and kicked it with his spurs: "I'm going to Bethlehem by myself. I don't want any company! I've had enough!"

"I want to go with you!"

Oh it's swell, it's swell, it's swell . . .

"Enough!"

Oh, it's swell, it's swell, it's swell . . .

(The voices get softer, as if they are disappearing into the distance.)

"Enough!"

Oh, it's swell . . .

"Enooooough!"

At that moment in the star-studded sky there appeared an archangel with a huge halo on his head, with large feathered wings that were beating so furiously that they slapped the clouds. And the fluttering of the air inflated the folds of his gown like a sail in a storm! He held a big bright sash in front of him, on which was written the word ANGEL, in case anyone wasn't sure!

He went circling through the sky shouting: "Men of good will, come! Come! The redeemer is born!"

And he flew down towards the ground in a nosedive—
BRUAAMMMM!

(He performs the angel's nosedive, which hurls him toward the ground and sends him zipping along, grazing its surface.)

And the shepherds shouted: "Oh, you miserable wretch, you're scaring the milk out of our sheep!"

(He performs another angel's nosedive, from which he barely manages to pull up.)

(In a booming voice) "The Savior is born—BRUAMMM!"
(An enraged reaction from the shepherds) "I hope you crash into a mountain, and your big halo gets caught around your neck and chokes you! And your feathers are scattered all over the place! You big chicken!"
(Turning back to the shepherds) "We better go right away to bring some gift to this infant Son of God, because if this big angel keeps flying back and forth all night, he'll plow up our fields."
And they all set out with a gift in a procession. One brought some cheese, one brought a baby goat, some rabbits, another some chickens, one brought some wine, some oil, baked apples, and chestnut pies . . . and then some of them showed up with huge buckets overflowing with polenta . . . *(Indicates a great weight)* and headed down from the mountain like this . . .
"How inappropriate—who ever heard of giving polenta to a newborn baby! Do you want to kill him?"
And in front of the manger there was an incredible racket. *(Describing it with gestures and rhythms that are almost a dance)* There were men sawing wood—BRA BRA BRA! Others were hammering on a blacksmith's anvil—BRIU BRA BRIU BRA BRA! Near them were some servants pumping the bellows that were blowing air— HAHA HEHE HA! —And to add some counterpoint to the cacophony there was the chorus of the marketplace . . .

(He executes a grammelot with voices of greengrocers, butchers, bakers, etc., rising to a grand crescendo of gibberish:)

(To the noisy marketplace) That's enough! Shame on you! That poor woman, the Madonna! She hasn't slept for three days and nights! Are you trying to kill her?

"But we just wanted to make the Nativity scene!"

And inside the manger were the shepherds who entered with their gifts and Saint Ann who saw them and said: "Go pray outside . . . hurry up and give me the gifts!" *(Mimes collecting and organizing the presents)* "Pray later. Oh look at all this stuff! Blessed baby Jesus . . . You should be born at least four times a month. I'll stockpile enough to last for all eternity!"

And the three Magi arrived with gold, incense and myrrh, and got down on their knees. There was the old Magus carrying his gift, then the young one, and then the black one came inside. *(Singing:)*

Oh it's swell, it's swell, it's swell
To see the baby's doing well!

"Get that black man out of here. He'll scare the baby!" shouted the old king.

Just then the angel with the spear of fire arrived and shouted: "Out! Get out immediately! Out, everybody clear out!"

"What do you mean clear out?"

"We're moving! They've got to escape! It's time for the Flight to Egypt!"

"Already?"

"Kind Herod is running around cutting off the heads of all the babies!"

Saint Ann said to Joseph: "Go get four horses and two carts and load them up with supplies right away!"

The angel: "No, there's no time for that. You have to leave immediately."

"Ah, nice try, you clever archangel. You want to take all this stuff for yourself, eh?" *(To Joseph)* "The donkey, the donkey, get the donkey!"

The donkey came out so loaded down that he could barely stand . . . he was out of breath after three days and nights of panting! *(Creates the panting of the animal)* Ahhh! Ahhh! He exploded! Saint Ann began loading everything onto its back: the gifts, the bundles, the packets, and when the Madonna climbed on as well, Joseph said: "Get down, Madonna, you don't want the poor thing to drop dead!"

"But I can't get down . . . because if the people don't see me on a donkey they won't understand that we're making the Flight to Egypt!"

So Joseph got under the donkey, and lifted up the beast, the Madonna, the child, and all the supplies onto his back and set out on the journey. Along the way he gave a shake and freed himself of all the presents. Walking, walking they went, reaching the sea coast, and then after many more footsteps and hoofprints they arrived in Jaffa. Jaffa, the big white city with tall towers.

As soon as they arrived at the gates, the angel made big circles in the sky and sounded his trumpet. The donkey—IAAAP!—belly on the ground. A fart—PLUUUF! The soul of the donkey went up to heaven! The Madonna looked at it and said: "Poor beast, it's dead. It's a sign from heaven. It means that we've arrived!"

They entered the city and looked for a covered shelter to sleep under. There was a miserable hovel, full of holes, that made the manger in Bethlehem seem like a palace.

The child fell asleep in the arms of his mother. And poor Joseph spent all night plugging up the holes.

In the morning when she woke up, the Madonna took a basket and went around looking for people who needed their laundry washed, because even she had to help the family survive. Saint Joseph also made the rounds with his tools, a hammer and saw, looking for work. And the child was left out in the street.

In the evening the mother returned from the washing place with her back bent. She sat down soaking wet and exhausted. And Saint Joseph came home in a rage because he had not found work; he hadn't hammered a single nail.

The child Jesus arrived with snot in his nose . . . dripping down to his mouth, dressed in rags, with filthy hands, pants falling down, without even any shoes on his feet: "Mamma, I'm hungry!"

"But look what a mess you've made of yourself, child . . . with all the work I have, now I have to wash *your* clothes too!"

"Mamma, I'm hungry!"

"But let me finish. I'm talking to you! Aren't you ashamed to come home in such a mess?"

"Mamma, I'm hungry!"

(Speaks with the words falling over one another as if it were a grammelot of gibberish) "Jesus Christ . . . is that any way to talk to . . . Ave Maria . . . you little brat . . . mamma mia, pasta fagiol . . . wait till I tell your father . . . dominus patris . . . hallelujah, hallelujah . . . that's amore!"

Because when the Virgin Mary had a fit of anger she spoke pure Palestinian so quickly that you couldn't understand a word—

"Holy Mother of God!" *(Changes tone)* "Joseph, will you explain to him that he has come down from heaven to teach good Christians to love and be kind and that the first love that he should show is respect for his mother . . ." *(To the child)* "And you, aren't you ashamed of yourself?"

"Oh, Jesus!"

"Joseph, did you hear how your son answered me? Can you please teach him some manners!"

"Me?"

"Of course—you're his father!"

"Me . . . his father?!" *(Rolls his eyes, perplexed)*

Finally the family began their dinner, all together sitting around the table. There was bread in the middle. The child began to reach out his hand . . .

"Eh, always grabbing with the hands right away! Wait! Look at those filthy hands! And make the sign of the cross first! No, wait . . . it's too soon! Another time!"

The child went to sleep, and the whole family slept.

In the morning Jesus woke up. His mother wasn't there. His father was gone. He put on his trousers, took a chunk of bread, and went out into the street. There were lots of children running around, jumping, playing. "Can I play too? . . . Let me play . . . I know how!"

"Go away, Palestinian!"

"But why won't you let me play? Look . . . I know how to play horsey . . . I can play cops and robbers too . . . and patty-cake."

"Get lost, hillbilly."

Streams of tears flowed down from his eyes . . . the child Jesus was overcome with sadness.

His mother had warned him: "Be careful. Don't make any miracles or the soldiers will hear about it, come looking for you, find you, and kill you!"

But the pain of finding himself chased away from the games was so sharp and deep that he couldn't stop himself from trying out a little miracle . . . to earn a little bit of their friendship. And he went to where there was a fountain surrounded by mud and clay . . . the kind used for making tiles and bricks, pretty, thick and wet. He grabbed a fistful and began working with his little holy hands, and he shouted: "Hey, kids, come over here and I'll show you how to make birds out of mud!"

(Mocking him) "Oh, the Palestinian is making birds out of mud!"

"Yes, but then I'm going to make them fly too!"

(Imitating him) "Eh, the Palestinian is going to build birds out of mud and then make them fly! Bravo!"

All the children came around to watch and make fun of him. And he began with his little holy hands—he made a rough version of the little head, then the wings, the little belly, delineating the feathers with a small stick. He took two twigs and stuck them in under the belly of the sparrow to make the legs. He held it up in his hand. "Without tricks or preparation, without even an oration—one, two three, blow!" *(Blows forcefully on the bird)*

He blew and the little mud bird shivered, a tremor. *(Puts his two hands together and moves them, giving the illusion that the sparrow has taken flight)* It spreads its wings and then starts to flap them—PIU PIU PIU PIU . . .

"It's flying! It's flying! It's a miracle! Jesus, the Palestinian boy made a mud bird fly!"

"Don't be ridiculous! That trick is as old as the Madonna! The trickster takes a bird that has fallen out of a tree, soaks it in water, and then smears it with mud as if he was the one who shaped it. Then he puts his hand over it—FIUM—a breath, its tail quivers—CIP CIP CIP—and it flies away!"

"No—it's true! It wasn't a little birdie smeared with mud. It wasn't a trick! I saw it myself. End of discussion! Watch this . . . I'm going to pick up another handful of mud!" *(Grabbing a lump of earth and splitting it in half)* "Look at that . . . there's nothing inside, no other bird in there! Now, go ahead Palestinian, do it . . . make a little bird . . . and don't try any tricks . . . you better not make me look bad or I'll punch you in the face!"

The child Jesus, with his little holy hands, outlined the shape of another little statue. "Let's hope I can do it again this time!"

He finds a little stick for marking the feathers . . . then two twigs for the legs. *(Quickly creating the new statuette)* "One, two, three, without tricks or preparation, without even an oration . . ."

At that moment a boy came forward from the back of the crowd. He had black eyes and curly hair: "Stop."

"What is it?"

"I'm checking to be sure!"

"Who are you?"

"Thomas."

"Thomas, you're starting early in the morning to bust my balls!"

Thomas took a nail—TIUM TIUM—and put a hole in the statuette. "Okay, there's no monkey business, you can go ahead!"

"One, two, three, without tricks or preparation, without even an oration . . ." *(Blows on the little bird)*

FIUM! The little bird opens its wings . . . it comes alive—PIU PIU PIU!

"It's flying! A miracle! Oh, what a phenomenon! What a marvelous wizard! Bravo, Palestinian! Darling, oh how

I love you!" *(With the tone of a sacred investiture)* "From this moment forward the child Jesus is the leader of the games! Now let's go get clumps of mud and make lots of birds any way we want them! Then he's going to breathe, make them fly and give us all a good laugh!"

And they were off, this gang of kids! Chirping like baby chickens and wild with joy they started building, and came up with birds like you've never seen before! There was one who took a lump of clay, improvised a fat rooster with a big head, a huge belly, with a little tail so tiny you could hardly see it. Then he stuck in a twig for a leg, another leg, but it fell forward. Another leg, it fell backwards, onto its ass!

"Let's give it five legs!"

"Don't get carried away! I never saw a bird with five legs!" said Jesus.

"All that matters is that it flies!"

Another one made a sausage-shaped snake with twelve wings all around it, and no tail, and no legs either. There was another child who made one in the shape of a big fat turd—you couldn't tell where its head was! Another made two little turds. Still another one made a cake with wings all around it and a head in the middle. The last one sculpted a cat—a pretty one—with wings.

"I can't make cats fly!"

"If you can make that big turd fly, you can make my cat fly, too!"

"No, we can't make cats fly—we have to draw the line somewhere!"

(The cat maker raising his voice) "Mamma! Jesus the Palestinian won't make my cat fly!"

(The mother leaning out her window) "Palestinian, you better make my little boy's cat fly or I'm going to come down there and nail you up!"

(The child with the fat rooster stretches out his hands and looks at the rooster in dismay.)

The child Jesus lifts up the fat rooster . . . breathes on it. *(Little by little the monstrous bird is brought to life)* PFFUUU

QUAQ QUIC QUOC QUA TE PU QUA! The sausage—PICI PETE TE CHE SI TEPE! The cake—PSE PSU PSU! The big turd—PETE TE CHE SI TEPE! The little turds—PCE PCI PQUE! The cat—PFUUUM GNIAAAOOOO GNIAAMM— it eats all the other birds in the sky!

"Oh how beautiful! It's so funny you could drop dead laughing!"

"Another round of birds. Let's make them all together."

Everybody was kneading clay into birds, playing, bursting into howls of laughter, singing! And the mothers leaning out from their windows laughed contentedly: "This Jesus is a good kid. He's found a game that's lots of fun, and they don't even hurt themselves!"

But at that moment—TRAK!—the gates of the piazza swung open and a little boy came through on a black pony with silver-and-gold saddling. The child had neatly combed hair, feathers in his hat, clothes made of silk and velvet, with a lace collar. With him were two armed henchmen riding two white horses. He was the son of a landowner, the richest man in the city.

"Hey, kids, what game are you playing?"

(The townspeople, whispering to Jesus) "It's the master's son . . . what a ball-breaker! Don't pay any attention to him, Palestinian. Pretend he's not there!"

"Can I play in your game, too?"

"No!"

"And why not?"

"Because you never even let us take a little ride on your ponies! And every time we come to your house where you have lots of big toys, you have your body guards throw us out! Now we're having lots of fun playing the greatest game in the world and the Palestinian is the leader of the game. You're rich, but you don't have the Palestinian! The Palestinian is ours! Isn't that right, Palestinian? Palestinian, don't have anything to do with that one—don't be a Judas!"

"But can you at least tell me what the game is?"

"Yes . . . we're making birds, birds out of mud . . . and then the Palestinian blows on them and makes them fly.

Do you want to play, too? Pull down your pants, blow on your little bird, and let's see it fly!"

And everyone laughed. But the son of the landowner didn't laugh. Purple with rage, his eyes popping out of his head, he grabbed a spear from one of the soldiers, and shouting like a madman, he dug his spurs into his horse who charged into the crowd of children: "If I don't play, nobody plays!"

ZAN ZAN—the hooves of the horse trampled over all the clay statuettes. The children exploded in a fit of wailing . . . they threw balls of muck at the nasty little boy, but the soldiers, making a carousel with their galloping horses, shouted: "Go away! Get out of here! Get lost, go! He can do whatever he wants, because he's the boss's son."

The mothers at the window: "Bastards! Such a nice game—that didn't cost anything—our children were happy!"

And the soldiers: "Go away, women! Go away or we'll hurl our spears."

PFIUM PFIUM—all the windows closed in a flash. In an instant the piazza was empty. There remained only the son of the landowner on his black horse with his snickering soldiers. No one noticed that the child Jesus was still there next to the fountain, with his big eyes full of tears . . . fixed on the sky that was full of clouds . . . and he began to call his father. The moment he called his father all life came to a stop—time stopped—everyone was frozen in stillness like statues: "DADDDEEEEEE!"

The clouds moved swiftly in a swirling circle . . . that opened up and left a huge void in the middle—BROOMMM!

"DADDDEEEEEE!"

(As if sticking his head out through the big void between the clouds) "What is it?"

"Father, it's me . . . your son, Jesus the Palestinian!"

"I recognize you! What happened to you?"

(Having difficulty holding back his tears) "Ehhh, that boy there is evil. He broke all the little mud statues that we made to play with . . ."

"My dear boy, for a silly little thing like that, did you have to scare your father out of his wits? I came running

all the way from the other side of the universe. I punc-
tured almost two hundred clouds, knocked over fifty
cherubs, and threw the triangle on my head so far out of
balance that it will take an eternity to get it on straight
again! Aren't you ashamed of yourself?"

(Sniveling with his voice pushed to falsetto by emotion)
"Eh . . . but he was mean . . . he smashed all the toys . . .
we were happy . . . he broke everything . . . I worked so
hard. Look!"

"I didn't understand a word you said! Speak clearly.
What happened?"

*(With great velocity, still interrupting the words with
sniffles)* "What happened is that Mamma and Joseph, too,
we all came to Jaffa . . . they went out to work . . . ehhh . . .
and I was all alone . . . ihhh . . . and then I went . . . to the
piazza . . . there were children . . . ahhh . . . they were
playing and I said: 'Can I play, too?' 'Go away Palestinian
hillbilly!' But I . . . ihhh . . . I couldn't, I didn't want to be
left out of the game . . . I was so sad . . . I wanted to die . . .
ahhh . . . and then I thought . . . I'll make a miracle . . . a
little one . . . the one that makes birds fly is easy and
always works for me . . . ahhhh . . . I made some awfully
big birds fly . . . and a little turd too, a big turd, and even
a cat . . . after that they were happy! One said: 'It's not
true . . . that Thomas is a ball-buster' . . . ahhh . . . and
they all said: 'Bravo, Palestinian, leader of the games.'
And now I'm just like I was before . . . because all my
friends ran away . . . ehhh . . . it hurts, Father . . . it hurts
so much!" *(Huge sniffles and tremendous sighs)*

"Oh, you are absolutely right. I have to admit that
destroying games as gentle as dreams—smashing toys
shaped by the imagination—is truly the worst of all sins.
But try to be reasonable and think about it. He's a little
boy. He doesn't understand."

"No, no . . . he understands, he understands! That one
was born evil. It would be very dangerous to let him grow
up!"

"All right, let's punish him. What punishment do you
want me to give him?"

(With the attitude of a satisfied child who tries to come up with an earth-shattering sentence) "Kill him!"

(Silence. One imagines that the Heavenly Father is shocked) "Ah . . . that's a nice start! I send you down to Earth from heaven to spread peace among men. To speak of love to people who usually beat each other like crazy, so that you can tell who the good Christians are right away by the fact that when one of them gets slapped, he immediately turns his face to get hit on the other cheek. And so they slap each other silly from morning to night, and are as happy as gods in heaven! Everything's going along 'marvelously' and—ZOM—you show up and right off the bat: 'Kill him!' Aren't you ashamed of yourself?"

"Eh, but he was mean . . . he made me cry!"

"But why are you calling me to give out punishments? You're God, too . . . a little one, a tiny Godini, but still God. Why do you have to put me in the middle of this judgment? Ha—I know very well why! You want me to pass judgment so the people will say: 'The Father is mean, but the Son is kind!' No, you untangle your own problems and don't bother me anymore with this kind of nonsense, because I have plenty of other things to do!"

BRAAAAMMMM! All the clouds gathered together in a big cluster, and the sky became clear. The little boy, the son of the landowner, laughed again and the henchmen snickered till they peed in their pants.

The Son of God approached the little master and said: "You're laughing, eh? Because you're so sure that no one can punish you, eh? . . ." *(Changes tone)* "And if someone showed up who could punish you?"

"Who would that be?"

"Me for example! . . . I'm too small? I don't have enough strength to punish you? Oh, yeah? And what if I hit you with a lightning bolt? . . . Ha . . . you don't believe me, eh?"

BRUAMMM—a flash of fire flew out of his eyes that enveloped the son of the landowner and tossed him up into the air—VUM—it burst into a blazing flame . . . the boy was transformed into a mud puppet that baked in a roaring furnace . . . red, yellow, orange. A little boy made of steaming hot clay!

The henchmen: "Ahhaa! The son of the devil!" They ran away.

All the women opened their windows: "A wizard! Son of the devil!" And they closed their shades.

The Madonna, who was at the washing place rinsing out clothes, hears the shouts: "Ah, witchcraft! . . ." She came running and arrived at the courtyard: "Jesus, my dear little son, what happened? Why are people shouting at the top of their lungs?"

"I don't know. We were here playing . . . Look, Mamma, I made my first miracle . . . and it's still hot!"

"A mud baby? Did you make it yourself?"

"No, no, that's him, just the way he was born . . . He was nasty. He insulted me awfully . . . After he smashed all the toys that I made out of mud . . . a flash of fire—all burnt up! Terracotta!"

"What? But aren't you ashamed of yourself? God, you're cruel! Think of what will happen when they carry this terracotta child to his mother. On her knees . . . the tears of blood that will fall! And they'll say: 'It was the Son of God, the Palestinian . . .' That's a nice start!" *(Sternly)* "Resuscitate him!"

"No!"

"Resuscitate him this instant!"

"Look . . . Can't I do anything, without having to undo it right away! Besides, I don't know how . . . I only learned how to throw lightning bolts . . . I don't know how to resuscitate yet, Mamma!"

"Don't tell lies. Do it for me . . . For my eyes, for the pain that pierces my heart!" *(Imploringly)* "Have pity!"

"Mamma, don't cry . . . stop shedding tears. I'll resuscitate him—but with a kick!"

(Jesus gives a terrible kick to the boy, who is stretched out on the ground.)

PAM—a kick at the boy that knocks the landowner's son straight back up on his feet . . . all the dirt crumbles off of him. The blood starts flowing in his veins . . . he breathes, he breathes, he's alive . . . his eyes open guardedly . . . he puts his hand on his buttocks.

"Don't worry . . . you're alive!"

(Stunned by his awakening) "What happened?!"

"I hit you with lightning. And then—thanks to the Madonna—! You feel a pain in your butt, eh? That ought to teach you that you can't earn your living by being arrogant all the time . . . because one day a poor little ragamuffin is going to show up and punish you with a kick in the ass, for all the others!"

Suddenly the sky became limpid and clear. The mothers came back to lean out of their open windows. Everyone looked into the distance towards the valley from which they could hear strange shouts. They could make out a tiny figure, a black man on a gray camel followed by an old white man digging his spurs into a black horse. One was singing and the other was shouting:

Oh it's swell, it's swell, it's swell
To be riding a camel
Oh it's swell, it's swell, it's swell . . .

"That's enough!"

Oh it's swell, it's swell, it's swell . . .

"That's enough!"

(The rhythmic duet gets louder and then diminishes as it disappears into the distance.)

THE MORALITY PLAY OF THE BLIND MAN AND THE CRIPPLE

On several occasions we have demonstrated how in the ancient popular theatre, texts with numerous roles have been performed by a single giullare who interprets all the characters one after the other. It is also the case in the dialogue we will present shortly, that two giullari can be interpreted by a single mime/performer. *(A slide is projected)* But often, in particular during the Middle Ages, the dialogue of "The Morality Play of the Blind Man and the Cripple" was presented on the stage by two separate performers. Arturo Corso, my collaborator for many years, has in fact taken this approach in Belgium where he staged "The Blind Man and the Cripple" with two different actors from the Flemish company Nouvelle Scène. The give-and-take of the dialogue between the blind man and the cripple worked wonderfully when it was performed in this way by a couple.

It is known that the pieces performed by the giullari in the Middle Ages were also called "moralities" and so it is not by chance that this grotesque piece unfolds to reveal a moral of the noblest intentions. The theme in question concerns the dignity of earning one's living. The key of the story is simple, almost elementary: a blind man, abandoned by his dog, finds himself in the middle of the street in a state of desperation, and without knowing what to do, asks for help. He is answered by someone as unfortunate as he is: a cripple who drags himself around on a rolling cart, who is also asking for help; unfortunately the wheels of his cart were broken off when they got stuck in the tracks of a carriage. So the blind man, following the voice of his unlucky companion, finds him and has an ingenious idea: he will carry the lame man on his shoulders, so that he will see through the eyes of the cripple who will in turn be able to walk thanks to the legs of the blind man. The cripple is delighted by this stupendous plan of his comrade and already predicts that they might be able to evoke a great sense of pity in the passersby who come upon this tragic marriage of misfortunes: this vision will induce them to be more generous in offering their charity.

The version that we are performing is very similar to the French version by André de la Vigne, satiric author of the late fifteenth century. Many other versions are known, all with different variations, but each of them focuses on the theme of dignity that we are highlighting. When the blind man and the cripple see Christ offstage in the distance, tied to a stake and being beaten, they have pity on him. And that is where the reversal of the moral begins.

—

VERSION FOR TWO GIULLARI

The Blind Man is on the right of the stage. The Cripple is on his knees on the opposite side.

BLIND MAN: Help me, good people. Give your charity to me, to poor, unfortunate me, bereft of both eyes. But maybe it's not so bad that I can't see, because I would be so moved by compassion that I would be in danger of driving myself mad.

CRIPPLE: Oh, kindhearted people, have pity on me. I am so ill-formed that when I look at myself it terrifies me so much that I would run away in leaps and bounds if I weren't so crippled that I can't move without a cart.

BLIND MAN *(Mimes walking into a column)*: TOCK! Ahi, I can't keep going around banging my head into every column in the neighborhood . . . help me, someone!

CRIPPLE: Ohi—I can't get myself out of this carriage track, because it broke the wheels off my cart, and I'll end up dying of hunger in here if no one helps me out.

BLIND MAN: I had a wonderful dog that used to go with me everywhere . . . but he ran away after some bitch in heat . . . at least I think the dog was a female, because I couldn't see it and I can't be sure . . . it could have been a vicious dog or a hairy cat that seduced him away from me. *(With a tone of increasingly tearful lamentations)* Help me! Help me!

CRIPPLE: Help, help . . . doesn't anybody have four new wheels they could lend me for my little cart? Lord God, grant me a blessing of four wheels!

BLIND MAN: Who's that wailing that he wants God to give him wheels?

CRIPPLE: It's me, the deformed cripple with the broken wheels.

BLIND MAN: Come closer to me, on the other side of the street, and I'll see what I can do to help . . . not that I can see anything . . . not without a miracle. But anyway, let's see!

CRIPPLE: I can't come over there . . . May God curse all the wheels in the world and turn them square so they don't roll anymore.

BLIND MAN: Oh, but if I could make my way over step by step to where you are . . . you can be sure that I'd be able to lift you all the way up onto my shoulders . . . except for your wheels and cart! We could transform ourselves into a single creature made out of the two of us . . . and satisfy each other's needs at the same time. I could get around with your eyes and you with my legs.

CRIPPLE: Oh, what an idea! You must have a gigantic brain, filled with wheels of all sizes. *(Stretches his arms out toward the heavens)* Oh, the Lord God has blessed me by lending me the wheels of your brain that will allow me to continue going around asking for charity!

BLIND MAN: Keep talking so I can orient myself. *(He gets closer)* Am I going in the right direction?

CRIPPLE: Yes, nice and easy, you're on the right track.

BLIND MAN: I'd better get down on all fours so I don't trip. Ahoy, should I head starboard?

CRIPPLE: Lean a little to the left . . . No! Don't get carried away! That's a turnabout . . . Heave anchor and come 'round again . . . That's it . . . pull out the oars, up with the sails . . . straighten out, straighten out . . . That's it, you're almost in the harbor now.

BLIND MAN: Do you take me for a five-masted schooner? Stretch out a hand when I get close.

CRIPPLE: I'm stretching out both of them. Come on, come on . . . pretty mamma's boy . . . you're almost there . . . No! . . . Holy Moses! Don't drift away . . . straighten up to starboard . . . Oh, my ship to salvation!

BLIND MAN *(Miming having found his friend)*: Did I find you? Is it you? Is it really you?

CRIPPLE: It's me, you beautiful blind old buzzard. Give me a hug.

BLIND MAN: I'm so happy I can't keep my skin on, my darling cripple! Come here and let me carry you . . . get up on my shoulders . . .

CRIPPLE: Yes, I'll climb on . . . turn the other way . . . bring your back down lower . . . Heave ho! I did it!

BLIND MAN: Don't stick your knee in my back . . . you're crushing me.

CRIPPLE: Excuse *me* . . . it's the first time I've been on horseback; I'm not used to it. And you, be careful not to smash into something and knock me off, please!

BLIND MAN: You can be sure I'll treat you as carefully as if you were a sack of red turnips. And you, be a trustworthy guide—don't send me walking into any cow dung.

CRIPPLE: I'll pay attention, don't worry. By the way, you don't happen to have a piece of metal you can put into your mouth to bite onto with a pair of straps attached? It would make it easier for me to lead you around.

BLIND MAN: That's nice—now you take me for an ass? Oh, how heavy you are! How can I move when you're so heavy?

CRIPPLE: Walk! Don't waste your breath . . . *(Happy, spurring him on)* Ahrii! Trot, my pretty little blind buzzard, and pay attention. When I pull your left ear, you turn to the left, and when I pull—

BLIND MAN: I get it! I get it! . . . I'm not an ass. Oh! Dammit, you're too heavy!

CRIPPLE: Me heavy? What are you talking about? I'm a feather
... a butterfly!

BLIND MAN: A lead butterfly. If I let you fall on the ground, well
water would start gushing out of the hole, for God's sake!
Did you eat a steel anvil for breakfast.

CRIPPLE: You're crazy . . . I haven't eaten for two days.

BLIND MAN: Okay, but it's probably been two months since
you've taken a shit.

CRIPPLE: Yes, I'm all screwed-up. As God is my witness . . . it's
been at least six days since I've been able to relieve
myself.

BLIND MAN: Six days? At least two meals a day . . . that makes
a dozen platefuls. Oh, Saint Gerolamo, protector of
porters, I'm carrying around a warehouse stockpiled for a
year of famine. I'm sorry, but I'm going to put you down
here, so you can do your sacred duty and get rid of that
illegal load of contraband.

CRIPPLE: Stop—do you hear that commotion?

BLIND MAN: Yes, it sounds like people shouting and cursing!
What are they shouting about?

CRIPPLE: Go back a little so I can see them more clearly . . . *(He
imitates a coachman reining in his horses)* Slow down . . .
like this . . . that's it, now I see . . . they're shouting at him
. . . Jesus Christ!

BLIND MAN: Jesus Christ what?

CRIPPLE: Jesus Christ himself, in person . . . Jesus, the Son of
God!

BLIND MAN: Son of God? Which one?

CRIPPLE: What do you mean which one? The only son, stupid!
The holiest son . . . they say he works miracles, marvels.
He heals sicknesses, the worst and most awful ones in the
world, for those who welcome them with joyful souls. So
I guess we better clear out of this country.

BLIND MAN: Clear out? Why?

CRIPPLE: Because I can't accept this condition with happiness.
They say that if this Son of God passes by, all of a sudden
I'll be miracle-ized . . . and you, too, in the same way . . .
Think about it a little, what would happen if the two of us
were really misfortunate enough to be freed of our mis-

fortunes! Right away we'd be in a condition that would force us to find a way to earn a living.

BLIND MAN: I say we should go meet this saint, who will rid us of our cursed afflictions.

CRIPPLE: You really think so? You want to be miracle-ized . . . all right, then you'll die of hunger . . . because everyone will shout at you: "Go get a job!"

BLIND MAN: Oh, it makes me break into a cold sweat to think about it . . .

CRIPPLE: "Go get a job, you vagabond," they'll tell you, "or go to jail." And we'll lose the great privilege that makes us equal to our lords and masters, collecting taxes: they do it by taking advantage of loopholes in the law, and we do it by begging for charity. All of us are taking advantage of the suckers.

BLIND MAN: Let's get out of here, we've got to escape this meeting with the saint. I'd rather die. Oh, mamma mia . . . let's go . . . let's fly, let's gallop . . . grab onto my ears so you can guide me as far away as possible from this city! Let's get out of Lombardi while we're at it . . . Let's go to France, to a place where this Jesus Son of God will never ever set foot. Let's go to Rome!

CRIPPLE: Easy now, easy, my animated madman, or you'll knock me off onto the ground . . .

BLIND MAN: Oh, I beg you, save me!

CRIPPLE: Calm down . . . we'll save each other all together . . . there's no danger anymore, because the saint's procession has stopped moving.

BLIND MAN: What are they doing?

CRIPPLE: They've tied him to a column . . . and they're beating him. Oh, how they're beating him, those hotheads!

BLIND MAN: Oh, poor child . . . why are they beating him? What did he do . . . to those miscreants?

CRIPPLE: He came to talk to them about loving each other like brothers. But be careful that you don't let yourself feel too much compassion for him, because it might increase your chances of getting miracle-ized!

BLIND MAN: No, no, I have no compassion . . . he's nobody to me . . . this Christ . . . I never even met him . . . but tell me, what are they doing now?

CRIPPLE: They're spitting on him . . . ugly pigs. They're spitting in his face.

BLIND MAN: And what is he doing . . . what is he saying, this miserable Son of God?

CRIPPLE: He's not saying anything . . . he's not speaking . . . he's not resisting . . . and he's not looking at those wretches with any anger . . .

BLIND MAN: And how is he looking at them?

CRIPPLE: He's looking at them with sadness . . .

BLIND MAN: Oh dear child . . . don't tell me anything else about what's happening because it's wrenching my guts . . . it's chilling my heart . . . and I'm afraid I'll say something that sounds compassionate.

CRIPPLE: Me, too. I feel a breath that chokes my throat and there are goosebumps on my arms. Let's go, let's get out of here!

BLIND MAN: Yes, let's go hide someplace where it won't be possible for us to discover our compassion for his suffering. I know a tavern . . . .

CRIPPLE: Listen!

BLIND MAN: What?

CRIPPLE: That big commotion over there . . .

BLIND MAN: Is it the Holy Son coming?

CRIPPLE: Oh God, spare me from fear because we are lost . . . No one's there near the column . . .

BLIND MAN: Not even Jesus Son of God? Where did they chase him?

CRIPPLE: They're here! The whole procession is coming this way. We're sunk!

BLIND MAN: Is the saint with them?

CRIPPLE: Yes, he's in the middle . . . and they've given him a heavy cross to carry, the poor thing . . .

BLIND MAN: Don't start losing yourself in compassion . . . better to hurry up and guide me someplace where we can hide from his eyes . . .

CRIPPLE: Yes, let's go . . . lean to starboard . . . run, run, before he can look at us, that miracle-izing saint . . .

BLIND MAN: Ohi—I twisted my ankle . . . I can't move anymore.

CRIPPLE: Oh, curse you with cankers! Now of all times? Can't you watch where you're putting your feet?

BLIND MAN: Eh, no I can't watch . . . because I've got no eyes so I can't see my feet! *(Interrupting himself; with astonishment)* What do I mean I can't? If they're there I can see them . . . I see them!!! *(Almost in ecstasy, he discovers all the parts of his body)* I see my feet! Oh what a beauteous pair of feet I have! Holy, pretty . . . with all those toes . . . so many toes! Five on each foot . . . and with the big nails and the little nails all lined up in order, from the hugest to the tiniest! *(He addresses his feet)* Oh, I want to kiss you all, one at a time. *(He bends over)*

(The Cripple is thrown to the ground.)

CRIPPLE *(Screaming while he falls to the ground)*: You, fool . . . behave yourself or you'll knock me off. Ohi—you murdered me! You miserable wretch . . . Do you want a kick—take that! *(He kicks him)*

BLIND MAN *(Doesn't respond to the kick, ecstatic over what he sees)*: Oh how marvelous . . . I can see the sky too . . . and the trees . . . and the women! *(As if he is watching them pass by)* Beautiful women! . . . Well, not all of them!

CRIPPLE *(A moment of wonderment)*: Was that me who kicked you? *(Pause. Astonishment)* Let me try again. Yes! Yes! *(Desperate)* What a cursed day this is! I'm ruined!

BLIND MAN *(Inspired)*: Blessed be that Holy Son who healed me! I see things that I've never seen in my life . . . I was a wretched beast to try to escape from him, because there is nothing more sweet and joyous in the world than light.

CRIPPLE: Would that the devil had carried him away along with all those who are grateful to him. Why did I have to be jinxed with the bad luck to be looked at by that love-soaked saint? I'm desperate! I'll die of empty intestines . . . Damn these resurrected legs. I'm so angry I could eat them raw.

BLIND MAN: Now I can see clearly what a fool I was to avoid the good path by keeping myself in darkness . . . because I didn't know what wonders I would see. Oh what beautifully colored colors . . . the eyes of the women . . . their lips . . . and all the rest! How beauteous are the ants and the flies . . . And the sun . . . I can't wait for the night so I can see the stars and go to the tavern to discover the color of wine! Blessed be the Lord, Son of God!

CRIPPLE: Oh poor me . . . now I will have to give my sweat and blood to a master so that I can eat . . . Oh, damned misfortunate—misfortune and rotten luck . . . I'll have to go around looking for another saint who will grant me the blessing of crippling my shanks again.

BLIND MAN: Wondrous Son of God . . . there are no words in the vernacular or in Latin that can describe your charity . . . it is an overflowing river! Bent over under a cross, you still have enough love in abundance to think of the misfortunes of we misfortunates.

VERSION FOR SOLO GIULLARE

Giullare begins in the role of the Blind Man.

GIULLARE: Help me good people . . . give your charity to a poor misfortunate soul, blind in both eyes, and a good thing it is that I can't see, because if I could, I would be so overwhelmed with compassion that I would drive myself mad. Help me! Help a lost soul . . . *(Bumping into a column)* Ahia! Shit! That column! Help me, I'm drunk . . . *(Bumps into another column)* TON! STON! Ohio! Another column! Help me! *(Another column)* TON! *(Desperate)* I'm surrounded by columns, a prisoner of columns! Give me a hand . . . because I've lost the dog that used to guide me . . . no . . . no, I didn't lose him, he ran away from me . . . I had him tied to a rope . . . and he yanked me over . . . and that debauched, degenerate dog went running after a bitch in heat, all excited, drunk . . . that's all they think about, those dogs! Well, at least I think it was a bitch in heat that made him delirious, but it could also have been a depraved cat, one of those that goes around seducing the dogs of blind men like me—who no one helps! *(Bumping into yet another column)* PAM! Ohi—I'll never get out of this trap! I can't keep going around banging and re-banging my skull into all these columns all over the neighborhood . . . *(In a plaintive voice, more than desperate)* Someone help me! *(Leans against a wall, then gets down on his knees)*

(In the role of the Cripple; almost in tears) Oh, good-hearted people, have pity on me, a person so deformed that when I look at myself it scares me so much that I would run away in leaps and bounds, if it weren't for the fact that I'm crippled . . . I can't move at all without this contraption, but my cart ended up stuck in these holes in the pavement and all four wheels were ruined. Help, help! Doesn't anyone have four new wheels to lend me? Lord God, grant me the blessing of four healthy wheels! God help me! If no one comes by to give me charity, how will I stay alive! Help me! Have mercy on me!

(Leans against the wall, assuming the character of the Blind Man) Who's shouting for mercy? Oh! I said it first, eh! Who is complaining that they want the wheels of God? Is it you?

(Another position change; as the Cripple) I'm the one complaining, the human deformity . . . The cripple . . . with the broken wheels. Do you recognize me?

(As the Blind Man) Yes, yes . . . Come close to me . . . over here to the other side of the street and I'll see if I can help you . . .

(From this point on, small gestures are enough to indicate the change of character.)

(As the Cripple) I can't, I have no way to get to you . . . May God curse all the wheels in the world and turn them square so they won't roll anymore! You come here . . . because I can't move without my little cart!

(As the Blind Man) But how can I make my way to where you are with all these columns blocking the path! May God curse all the columns in the world . . . and make them fall down on everyone's head like a storm! Damned columns! *(Changes tone)* I have an idea. The fury of these pillars smashing into my head has opened up my brain!

I could make my way straight to you . . . if you talked to me and stopped me when I was about to bump into a column . . . *(Speaks as if he were the Cripple)* "No, stop! There's a column there . . . go that way . . . slow down, there's another column . . ." I move forward . . . and I find you. Look, I could even lift you up on my shoulders, all of you, except for the wheels and the cart. We could transform the two of us into a single creature. I could carry you on my back as if you were in the cavalry on a horse . . . all of a sudden I become your legs and you become my eyes and we can go around together asking for charity with four hands! Charity! Charity! Charity! . . . We would make a wonderfully pitiful pair!

(As the Cripple) Ohi—what an idea! You must have a very large brain, filled with wheels of all sizes! *(Stretching his arms to the sky)* Ohi—the Lord God has granted me the blessing of lending me the wheels of your brain so I can go around and inspire even more pity from people than before!

(As the Blind Man) Keep talking so I can orient myself. *(Gets closer)* Is this the right direction?

(As the Cripple) Yes, keep going, you're on the right path.

(As the Blind Man) Should I keep going straight?

(As the Cripple) Yes, take it easy and I'll give directions.

(As the Blind Man) I'm coming . . . Help me . . . speak, say something . . . because I'm getting there. *(Stops; threateningly)* Ah, don't play tricks on a poor blind man, or else when I find you, I'll strangle you!

(As the Cripple) I told you to take it easy! Let's go! You can come forward without a care because there are no columns.

(As the Blind Man) Are you sure? There's no columns? *(He takes a step and mimes bumping into a column)* TON! But . . .

(As the Cripple) That was a tree!

(As the Blind Man; furious) I could tell also that it was not a column: it's a tree . . . but trees can also bust your skull! Dammit! You have to warn me! Not only about columns, but also about trees, posts and houses too! If

I want to stop smashing into things I'd better try the doggy position. *(He gets down on all fours; changing his tone)* I'm coming forward . . . can I? Should I move? Are you sure? I'm moving. *(He does. He stops. He sniffs his hand with disgust)* It's not a column, it's not a tree, but it stinks! It's shit! A turd! I'm taking another route. I don't trust your advice . . . *(He directs himself to the place where the Cripple should be by moving backward like a crab)* This way even if there's a column, a tree or a turd, I'll only hit it with my ass! Watch out, here I come!

(As the Cripple) Come, come to your mamma, pretty baby, come here, come dearie, don't be afraid! Don't float away . . . come straight to the starboard side . . . Oh, my ship to salvation! *(Proudly to himself)* I'm also a poet! Come, beautiful, come . . . Careful . . . careful . . . there's a pile of cow shit! You're right in the middle of it! I understand that you're blind in both eyes, but is your nose also so blind that it can't smell that stench! Oh, you poor wretch, you're shit-faced all over! Come here you little troublemaker . . .

(As the Blind Man; finally finding his friend) Did I find you? It is really you?

(As the Cripple) It's me, you beautiful blind buzzard of gold. Give me a hug! *(They hug)* Not with your hands! *(Wipes off his face with disgust)* Come here, dearie . . . so I can give you a kiss!

(As the Blind Man) I made it! I made it! Thank you Saint Christopher! Now get moving . . . climb up on my shoulders . . . give me your leg . . . your leg, not your arm! *(Stops himself, astonished)* Is that a leg? How disgusting! I'm happy to be blind so I don't have to look at it! Give me the other one . . . come on, come on . . . . My Lord! Good God . . . What are you? A rabbit? *(To himself)* Oh, what a shame! *(To his companion)* Come on, up you go, push up with your ass . . . come on, get that big ass up there! Ohi—you have the legs of a rabbit, but the ass of an elephant, eh! Mother of God! Let's go . . . push hard . . . that's it! Op, op . . . *(Angry)* No, don't stick your knee in my backbone, or you'll paralyze me . . .

(As the Cripple) Sorry, it's the first time I've been on horseback, I'm not used to it. Ohi—and you, be careful not to knock me off, please!

(As the Blind Man) Stop, stop! You're a regular ton of bricks!

(As the Cripple) Me, a ton of bricks? . . . Why I'm a feather . . . a butterfly?

(As the Blind Man) A lead butterfly, so heavy that if I dropped you you'd make a hole in the ground deep enough for water to come gushing out . . . Holy Moses! Did you eat an iron anvil for breakfast?

(As the Cripple) Are you crazy, I haven't eaten for two days.

(As the Blind Man) That's fine, but you probably haven't taken a shit for two months.

(As the Cripple) That's no idle boast . . . God is my witness . . . it's been six days since I've relieved myself.

(As the Blind Man) Six days? At least two meals a day, that makes twelve platefuls. Saint Gerolamo, protector of porters . . . I'm carrying around a warehouse that's stocked up for a year of famine. I'm sorry but I'm going to put you down here so you can do your holy duty and relieve yourself of that illegal contraband!

(As the Cripple) Stop blathering! *(Happy)* Ohi—what a beautiful horse you are, you eyeless wonder! Boogie woogie boogie . . . I'm on horseback! How sweet it is . . .

I want to buy a horse. *(Commanding him)* Trot, my beautiful blind buzzard! Hhiioooo!

(As the Blind Man) Don't hit me like that or you'll break my back!

(As the Cripple) Hey, listen: you don't happen to have a piece of metal to put in your mouth to bite on that we can attach to a couple of straps? It would make it easier for me to guide you around . . . I could pull you here . . . and pull you there and then . . . okay . . . I can do it with your ears . . . Pay attention: when I pull your left ear, you go to the left, and when—

(As the Blind Man) I know!

(As the Cripple) Stop! Don't you hear that commotion?

79

(As the Blind Man) Yes, it sounds like people yelling and cursing!

(As the Cripple) Who are they shouting at? Take a few steps back so I can get a better view *(Imitates a rider reining in his horse)* Whoaaa . . . easy boy! Okay, now I see . . . oh . . . Jesus Christ!

(As the Blind Man) Jesus Christ, what?

(As the Cripple) It's him . . . Jesus Christ in person . . . Jesus, the Son of God!

(As the Blind Man) Son of God? Which one?

(As the Cripple) What do you mean which one? The only son, you ignoramus.

(As the Blind Man) You mean to say that God only has one son? Poor guy!

(As the Cripple) They have him tied to a column . . . and they're beating him. Oh, how they're whipping him, those miscreants!

(As the Blind Man) Oh, that poor child . . . why are they beating him? What did he do to those bastards?

(As the Cripple) He came to teach them all to love each other like brothers. He's a holy-man-wizard without equal! They say he can make miracles, marvels—he heals the most awful sicknesses of the world for those who bear them with joyful souls. He feels compassion and love for you. He doesn't ask if you want it, he just straightens your leg, or makes you see out of your eye—he miracle-izes you, and that's it! But be careful about letting yourself feel compassion for him, because you run a big risk of being miracle-ized. Don't let yourself go, don't soften yourself with pity! We'd better make a getaway from this neighborhood.

(As the Blind Man) A getaway? Why?

(As the Cripple) I'm telling you that if this Son of God happens to pass by here, I'll be miracle-ized in a flash . . . and you, too, in the same way! TOCK!—miracle-ized, fucked-over and screwed! We'll be screwed! Don't you understand? I can't accept this condition with happiness. We'll have to work under a master, subject ourselves to curses and beatings . . . all of a sudden we'll find ourselves stripped of the greatest privilege that we enjoy!

(As the Blind Man) Oh . . . it makes me break out into a cold sweat just to think of it! You're right! The greatest privilege that we have is to be on an equal level with the lords and aristocrats, and collect taxes. They do it with their lawbooks and their swords . . . we do it with pity! If we're miracle-ized, we can say good-bye to begging!

(As the Cripple) Oh! Finally, you understand! Let's clear out of this place before that wizard gets his hands on us. We can go hide out in some hole, where this miracle-izer won't be able to find us! I know a tavern . . . run, run!

(As the Blind Man) No, we have to get further away than that! Out of the city. Let's go to Ferrara!

(As the Cripple) Ferrara! Okay, let's go . . . go, go, go! *(He stops in terror)* Stop! Jesus Christ will go to Ferrara too, I'm sure of it!

(As the Blind Man) Okay then, let's go to Bologna! Let's go, let's go to Bologna!

(As the Cripple; uneasy) Stop! He's going to Bologna too . . . Jesus goes everywhere!

(As the Blind Man) No! There's one city where he could never go! *(Pause)* To Rome! I'm sure he'll never make it to Rome! Let's go, let's go! *(Mimes slipping)* MUAH!—miserable wretch! Another big pile of cow shit! I slipped in it! Oh, I've gone lame . . . I can't move my foot anymore!

(As the Cripple) Curse you with cankers! Now of all times? Can't you watch where you put your hooves?

(As the Blind Man) How can I look where I'm going when I can't see! I can't see, I can't . . . *(Interrupts himself all of a sudden, astonished; he pauses)* Dammit! I can see!! Thank the Lord, I can see! *(Almost in ecstasy, he discovers everything that's around him, starting with his feet)* Ohooo . . . My feet! Look how pretty my feet are! One, two, three, four little toes . . . And what a beautiful big toe! . . . Look! The trees . . . the stones . . . Ohooo! Look, the grass with the little flowers . . . I want to bend down and pick one . . . *(He leans over, then:)*

(Falling to the ground in a heap as the Cripple) You miserable wretch, damn you! You made me fall to the ground! . . . *(Gives him a kick)* TOCK! *(A moment of*

astonishment) Was that me who just gave him a kick? Let me try that again . . . *(Another kick)* Yes . . . yes! *(Changes tone)* Stop kidding around! Who lifted my leg up from behind? Who pulled up my le— *(Interrupts himself; astonished, he pauses)* Two legs miracle-ized! Two legs in a single stroke! Christ, you got carried away! What a cursed day this is . . . I'm ruined!

(As the Blind Man, in ecstasy, continuing to look around) Look at the ants! Darling beauties! The flies . . . those must be the flies! Oh, what a big fly . . . no, that's a bird . . . two birds! The plants . . . that one has green leaves . . . so many leaves! Oh, so many leaves . . . One, two, three, four, five, six *(Continues to count very quickly, then stops himself, changing tone)* I'll count them later! *(Opens his eyes wide)* The women! Oh how beautiful women are! *(Still more entranced)* Oh, how beautiful women are! Vuah! *(A series of onomatopoeic sounds that signify his great appreciation. Then a long gaze at the "panorama")* . . . Well, not all of them! *(Inspired)* The sky, how deep the sky is . . . and how long it is too! Now I understand what color is . . . how wonderful! How the sun beats down! Oh, light, light, light . . . light that I can't look at without it making me drunk . . . that floods my brain! Thank you, Jesus! The greatest miracle you've given me is making me understand that there is no dignity in making your living by pulling pity out of people, asking for charity from those who sweat and slave away. It's better to subject yourself to a master, as long as your eyes and legs are healthy, and you can plot a way to pull the bloodsuckers off your back.

(As the Cripple) What kind of ridiculous talk is that. To have masters, but torture yourself to be free of them. No, that's not for me. *(Bristles with rage)* You miserable wretch . . . you'll understand when you're under the control of a master, being beaten . . . and when your woman has to sell herself as a whore, and your children are slaves, dying of hunger . . . you'll understand what dignity is. I won't accept that condition. I don't want this miracle. I demand to be turned back into what I was before—a

beggar! I want a life with little bread, but total freedom! *(Walking around like a crazy man; in a desperate voice)* Does anyone know a wizard who has a potion or who can make signs with his hands, with fire, with metal that will cripple my legs? Help me! Don't you know anyone, maybe a woman-witch . . . *(Crying)* Help me! Help me to cripple my legs like before! Jesus! Where are you? Jesus! Jesus, have mercy! I wasn't the one who cursed you! Jesus why have you condemned me? Jesus. Jesus.

THE MADONNA MEETS
THE MARYS

PROLOGUE

The piece that follows—a secular passion play that can be traced back to the ancient lauds of central Italy, particularly in Umbria— deals with another tragic situation.

It is about the Madonna who meets the Marys in the street as they are on their way to the market. She talks to them about shopping and prices. In the background, as crosses pass by, one hears shouting and insults. It is reminiscent of a famous painting by Brueghel in which we see Mary and the other women in the fore- ground. There is a market, there are street performers, there is par- tying, a lot of noise; and in the background, very tiny, one catches a glimpse of crosses passing by—the crucifixion—and it is all hap- pening as if it is forgotten, like an event of minor importance. Put- ting those scenes together is an astonishing dramatic invention.

The piece can be performed with the participation of several different actors playing the various roles. In our case we chose to follow the tradition of the medieval storytellers who succeeded in interpreting all the roles themselves in a solo performance. Franca will take on the difficult task of performing it in an invented lan- guage devised by the giullari of southern Italy.

VERSION FOR SOLO GIULLARE

Mary walks down the street. When she gets close to the marketplace she meets her friends Amelia and Giovanna.

GIULLARE: "Greetings, Giovanna, and good day to you, too, Amelia. Have you already done your shopping?"

(They make the usual small talk about prices going up for no reason. Suddenly they hear a commotion of yelling and shouting.)

"What's that?" asks Mary. "Where are all those people going? What's happening back there." *(Points offstage)*
"It must be a wedding celebration," says Giovanna.
"Yes, you guessed, it's a wedding," chimes in Amelia. "I was just coming from there now."
"Let's go see!" says Mary, and heads in that direction.
(Giovanna, stopping her) "No let's hurry on to the market."
"Come on, just for a minute . . . let me see it. I like weddings so much! Who's the bride . . . is she young? And the groom, do you know him?"
"I think it must be someone from out of town. Let's go, Mary . . . let's go back home, it's already time to put the water on the fire."
"Wait . . . listen . . . they're cursing, those ones there."
"They're cursing from happiness and contentment."
"No, it sounds like they're angry. 'Wizard' . . . they shouted . . . Yes, that's what I heard . . . listen, they're saying it again . . . Who are they mad at, Amelia?"
"Now I remember. They're not shouting for a wedding. They're yelling at someone they discovered last night dancing with a goat, who turned out to be the devil."
"Ah, that's why they're calling him a wizard!"
"Yes, that's why. But let's go home, because that's not a show we want to see . . . we might get cursed by the evil eye."

(Mary turns around and looks into the distance at the far end of the road and says breathlessly:)

"Look, there's a cross sticking up above the people's heads
. . . and there . . . another two crosses behind it."

(Giovanna, playing along) "Yes those other two are for
two thieves . . ."

"Nasty people . . . they're going to crucify all three of
them . . . Think of their mothers! And the poor woman
probably has no idea what's happening to her son."

*(At that moment Mary Magdalene runs toward them. Out
of breath she shouts:)*

"Mary! Oh, Mary! . . . your son . . . Jesus . . ."

(Giovanna silences her immediately with a shove) "Oh
yes, oh yes, she already knows . . ." *(Aside, to Mary
Magdalene)* "Be quiet, you fool!"

(And Mary) "What do I already know? What happened
to my son?"

"Nothing . . . what could possibly have happened to
your son . . . Holy Mother of God? It's just that . . ."
(Changes tone) "Oh, I didn't tell you yet? What a scatter-
brain I am! Your son asked me to tell you that he wouldn't
be coming home for lunch this afternoon . . . because he
has to go to the mountain and preach a few parables."

(And Mary, to Magdalene) "And this was the news that
you wanted to tell me?"

"Yes, that's it, Madonna."

"Bless the Lord, child! You came running so quickly,
so agitated, that my heart almost stopped beating from
fear. I was already imagining all kinds of disasters. Sometimes we mothers are so silly . . . every little thing sets us
shouting right away about a tragedy."

(Giovanna, making the situation worse) "Sure, but
then this one runs in like a crazy woman just to give you
this shitty piece of news."

"Calm down, Giovanna . . . don't yell at this young girl
. . . Don't forget that she only came to do me the favor of
passing on a message!" *(To Magdalene)* "What is your
name, anyhow . . . I have a feeling I know you?"

(Embarrassed) "I'm . . . My name is Magdalene . . ."

"Magdalene? Which one . . . that one? . . ."

(And Giovanna) "Yes, that one . . . the courtesan. Let's go, Mary. Let's go home, because it's better that we not be seen with certain people; it's not proper."

"But I don't practice that profession anymore."

"That's because you can't find any more lechers to ensnare! Get out of here you shameless floozy."

"No, don't attack her, poor thing. If Jesus had so much faith in her that he sent her to me carrying a message, it's a sign that she must have changed her ways . . ." *(To Magdalene)* "Is it true?"

"Yes, now I've changed my ways."

(Giovanna, quickly adding) "Sure, go ahead and believe her . . . the fact is that your son is too good . . . he lets himself get carried away with compassion . . . and everybody screws him! He's always surrounded by a bunch of good-for-nothings, loafers, without work or skills, dying of hunger—wretches and whores—just like this one!"

"Don't speak so cruelly, Giovanna! He, my son, always says that it's for them above all, for them—the lost and abandoned—it's for them that he came to this world . . . to restore their hope!"

"All right, but don't you understand that by carrying on like that, he's not making a good impression on people . . . They're whispering behind his back. With all the well-brought-up people that we have in this town—the lords with their ladies, the doctors, the merchants—and he with his gentle manners, erudition and wisdom could easily put himself in their good graces, and have their honor and help if he needed it. But, no! The rascal hangs around with parasites and peasants and opposes our finest citizens."

(Mary, distressed) "Do you hear how they're shouting and laughing. But you can't see the crosses anymore!"

(Giovanna, continuing her discourse) "Besides the fact that he could at least stop speaking out all the time against the priests and monsignors . . . they never forgive anybody."

(Mary looks beyond the walls) "Ah, you can see the three crosses again."

(Giovanna can't stop herself) "One day they're going to make him pay. They're going to hurt him!"

"Hurt my son? And why? As sweet as he is? Isn't he always doing good deeds for people, even the ones who don't ask for anything?" *(Still concerned with the clamor taking place in the distance)* "Listen, they're snickering again. One of the crosses fell down. Someone's ended up on the ground. Everyone loves my son . . . isn't it true? Tell me, Magdalene . . ."

"Yes, I love him, too!"

"Oh, we all know the kind of love you have for the son of Mary!"

"My love for him is no more than the love one has for a brother . . . now."

"Now! Why, what was it before?"

"Giovanna, stop tormenting the poor thing for a moment . . . What did she do to you? Can't you see she's mortified?" *(Changes tone, very agitated)* "Why are they shouting so much?" *(Returning to the dialogue)* "And even if she, this young girl, does have a love for him, a love for him that is like the love that girls normally have for men that they like, what of it? Isn't he a man maybe, my son . . . in addition to being God . . . He has the eyes, the hands, the feet of a man—he has everything that a man has— including sadness and happiness. So it is up to him, and him alone, to decide when he has arrived at his moment. If he wants to take her for his bride, as far as I'm concerned, I'll love her like my own daughter . . . or at least I'll make a good effort at it. And I'm really hoping that day will come soon, because he's already past his thirty-third birthday, and it's time that he settles down and makes a family." *(Distressed)* "What vulgar shouts they're making back there. And that cross is so black!" *(Returns to the conversation)* "Oh, I'd be so happy to have his babies around the house . . . his . . . to play with them, rock them to sleep, since I know a lot of lullabies and nursery rhymes. It would be so nice to spoil them and tell

them stories, the kind that always finish nicely with
happy endings."

"Yes, all right, but now come out of your dreams,
Mary. Let's go, because at this rate we won't even have
any food ready for dinner."

"I'm not hungry . . . I . . . I don't know why . . . I feel a
big knot in my stomach . . . I really have to go see what's
happening over there."

"No! Stop! We're not going there! It's a spectacle that
will end in sadness. The kind that will leave you with a
heaviness in your heart all day long. And your son would
surely not be happy about it. It could be that at this very
moment your son is home waiting for you—and he's
probably very hungry!"

"But if he sent a message to say he's not coming!"

"Well, maybe he changed his mind . . . you know how
sons are. When you're there waiting, they don't come
home, and then they pop up when you're not waiting
there anymore, so you have to always be ready with a
soup on the fire."

"Yes, you're right. Let's go." *(To Magdalene)* "Do you
want to come, too, Magdalene, and have a bowl of soup."

"With pleasure . . . if it's not too much trouble for you."

(At that moment, Veronica passes by in the distance.)

(Mary, asking) "What could have happened to that woman?
She has a bloody cloth in her hand." *(To Veronica, raising
her voice)* "Oh, my friend, are you hurt?"

"No, not me . . . one of the condemned men that was
put on the cross."

*(Mary, breathlessly, as if she knows what the answer will
be)* "Which one?"

"The one they were calling a wizard. But he's not a
wizard. He's a saint. You can see it from the sweet eyes he
has. I wiped off his bloody face."

"Oh, merciful woman."

"See, I wiped it with this napkin and a miracle happened.
It left an imprint of his face as if it had been painted there."

(Almost voiceless) "Let me take a look."

"Yes, I'll show it to you."

(Giovanna, trying to distract her) "No, Mary, let it go."

"I'll let you see it, but first, oh lady, make the sign of the cross."

(Veronica shows Mary the napkin. Mary falls to the ground senseless.)

(And Giovanna) "What are you doing? Can't you see that she's fainted?"

(And Veronica) "Oh, Jesus! What did I do? Why did she collapse like that? Is she a relative, of that one?"

(And Giovanna) "She's the mother! Mary, the Mother of God!"

VERSION FOR MULTIPLE GIULLARI

Walking down the street, Mary and Giovanna meet Amelia.

AMELIA: Good day, Mary . . . good day, Giovanna . . .

MARY: Hello, Amelia. Are you going to do some shopping?

AMELIA: No, I already did that this morning . . . I have something to tell you, Giovanna.

GIOVANNA: Tell me . . . *(To Mary)* Excuse me, Mary . . .

(They move away and confer.)

MARY *(Looking offstage)*: Where are all those people going? What's happening over there?

GIOVANNA: It must be some wedding celebration.

AMELIA: Yes, it's a wedding . . . I was just coming from there now.

MARY: Oh, let's go see, Giovanna. I love weddings so much. Is the bride young? And who is the groom?

GIOVANNA: I don't know . . . I think he's from out of town.

AMELIA: Let's go, Mary. We can't waste time on weddings . . .

let's go home. We still have to put the water on the fire for the soup.

MARY *(Apprehensively)*: Wait . . . listen . . . they're cursing!

GIOVANNA: Oh, they're cursing out of happiness and contentment!

MARY: No, it sounds like they're angry . . . they shouted "wizard" . . . if I heard right. Listen, they're saying it again. Who are they mad at?

GIOVANNA: Oh, now I remember . . . they're not shouting about a wedding, but against someone they found last night dancing with a goat . . . who turned out to be the devil.

MARY: Ah, is that why they're calling him a wizard?

GIOVANNA: Yes, that's why . . . but it's getting late, Mary . . . Let's go home, because there's nothing to see over there . . . and you could get cursed by the evil eye.

MARY *(With growing agitation)*: There's a cross sticking up over the heads of the people! . . . And now there's two more of them raised up.

GIOVANNA: Yes, those others are for two thieves . . .

MARY: Poor people . . . they're going to crucify all three of them . . . think about their mothers! The poor woman, she probably doesn't even know that they're killing her son.

(Mary Magdalene catches up to them, running and out of breath.)

MAGDALENE: Mary! Oh, Mary . . . your son Jesus . . .

GIOVANNA *(Stopping her)*: Yes, yes, she knows about it already . . . *(To Magdalene)* Be quiet . . . you wretch!

MARY *(With apprehension)*: What do I already know about? What's happened to my son?

GIOVANNA: Nothing . . . what could have happened to him? Holy Mother of God. It's just that . . . Ah, didn't I tell you? Oh, how absentminded I am . . . it slipped my mind that your son asked me to tell you that he wasn't coming home for lunch this afternoon . . . because he had to go to a mountaintop and preach some parables.

MARY *(To Magdalene)*: Is that all you were coming to tell me?

MAGDALENE: Yes, that's it, Madonna.

MARY: Well thank the Lord! You came running so quickly, dear girl . . . that I was frightened. I was imagining all kinds of disasters . . . How silly we mothers are! We're always worried about nothing!

GIOVANNA: Yes, but what about her, this hussy, who comes running over here, all hot and bothered, to give you this silly little bit of news . . .

MARY: Calm down, Giovanna . . . don't shout at her now. In the end she just came to do me the favor of delivering a message. *(To Magdalene)* I thank you, young lady . . . what's your name. It seems that I know you from somewhere?

MAGDALENE *(With humility and embarrassment)*: I . . . I'm Magdalene . . .

MARY: Magdalene? Which one? . . . *(Short pause)* That one . . .

GIOVANNA *(Aggressively)*: Yes, it's her . . . the courtesan! Let's get out of here, Mary. Let's go home . . . it's better for us not be seen with people like that . . . it's not proper!

MAGDALENE: But I don't practice that profession anymore.

GIOVANNA: That's because you can't find any more dirty old men to be your customers . . . Get out of here you shameless floozy.

MARY: No, don't chase the poor child away . . . If my dear Jesus had enough faith in her to send her to me with a message, it's a sign that she has changed her ways . . . is that true?

MAGDALENE: Yes, I've changed my ways now, Mary.

GIOVANNA: Go ahead and believe her . . . We all know that your son is too good. He gets carried away with compassion and everyone screws him! He's always surrounded by a crowd of good-for-nothings . . . people with no jobs or skills, dying of hunger . . . wretches and whores . . . *(Pointing to Magdalene)* Just like that one!

MARY: Don't be so nasty, Giovanna! He, my son, always says that it's for them, above all for them—the lost and abandoned—that he came to this world . . . to give them hope.

GIOVANNA: All right, but don't you understand that in this way he's not making a good impression on people? They're whispering behind his back! With all the well-brought-up people we have in this city—the cavalry officers and their ladies, the doctors and lords—he with his gentle ways, wisdom and erudition, could easily put himself in their good graces and gain their respect . . . get their help if he needed it. Not that rascal! He goes hanging around with lousy peasants! And opposes those fine citizens!

MARY *(Listening apprehensively to the noises coming from the distance)*: Listen to how they're shouting and laughing! And you can't see the crosses anymore!

GIOVANNA *(Trying to distract Mary)*: And besides that he could at least stop speaking out all the time against the priests and prelates—they never forgive anybody!

MARY *(Flinching)*: Look, there's the three crosses again!

GIOVANNA *(Not giving up)*: One day, they're going to make him pay! They're going to hurt him!

MARY: Hurt my son? Why? He's so kind . . . he does nothing but good deeds for everyone, even those who don't ask for anything! And everyone loves him! *(Changes tone; agitated)* Listen . . . they're snickering again . . . one of them must have fallen to the ground . . . you can't see the third cross anymore . . . *(Turning back to the women)* Everyone loves my son . . . isn't it true?

MAGDALENE *(Timidly)*: Yes . . . I love him very much, too!

GIOVANNA: Oh, everybody knows the kind of inspired love you have for the son of Mary!

MAGDALENE: I love him just like a brother—now.

GIOVANNA: Now . . . and how was it before? . . .

MARY: Giovanna, stop tormenting the poor girl! What did she do to you? . . . Can't you see she's mortified? *(Listens to the shouting in the distance)* Why are they shouting so much? *(Turns back to her friends)* And even if she, this young girl, did have a love for him, that was like the love that women normally feel for men they like . . . that would be fine! Isn't my son a man, in addition to being God? Doesn't he have the eyes, hands, feet, and everything else that a man has—including sadness and happiness! So it's up to him, my son, to decide. He'll know the right thing to do when his moment comes, if he wants to take a wife. As far as I'm concerned, whoever he chooses, I'll love her like a daughter. And I hope very much that this day comes soon, because he's already thirty-three

94

years old—it's time to settle down and have a family. *(Changes tone)* Oh, what ugly things they're shouting over there . . . and how black that cross is! *(Turning to the women)* I would love so much to have his children around the house, to play with them, rock them to sleep, since I know a lot of lullabies, and spoil them, and tell them stories, the kind of fairy tales that always turn out well—with a happy ending!

GIOVANNA: But now that's enough of your dreaming, Mary. Let's go, because at this rate we won't even eat by evening.

MARY *(Consumed with profound sadness)*: I'm not hungry, I . . . I can't figure out why, but, I'm getting a knot in my stomach . . . I think I have to go and see what's happening over there.

GIOVANNA: No, don't go! . . . Those kinds of things make you sad and leave your heart heavy all day long, and your son wouldn't like it. He could be home waiting for you at this very moment, and he's probably hungry.

MARY: But if he sent me a message that he's not coming!

GIOVANNA: Maybe he changed his mind. You know how sons are—when you wait for them, they don't come home, then they pop up when you're not waiting anymore! You always have to be ready with something to eat on the fire.

MARY: Yes, you're right . . . let's go . . . Do you want to come, too, Magdalene, and have a bowl of soup?

MAGDALENE: Yes, I'd like to, if it's not too much trouble for you.

(In the distance Veronica passes by.)

MARY: What happened to that woman . . . she has a napkin covered with blood? *(Raising her voice)* Oh, good woman . . . are you hurt?

VERONICA: No, not me . . . but one of the condemned men that they put on the cross . . . the one they called a wizard . . . and who isn't a wizard, but a saint! He must be a saint. You can see it from the sweetness in his eyes . . . I wiped off his bloody face . . .

MARY: Oh, merciful woman . . .

VERONICA: . . . with this napkin, and a miracle happened . . . he left the imprint of his face on it. It's like a portrait.

MARY *(Without breathing, almost foreseeing the tragedy that approaches)*: Let me see it . . .

GIOVANNA *(Agitated, trying to distract her)*: Don't be so curious, Mary—it's not polite!

MARY: I'm not curious . . . I just feel that I have to see it.

VERONICA: All right, I'll show it to you, but first make the sign of the cross . . . There, look—it's the Son of God!

MARY *(With a thin voice)*: It's my son! Ah . . . it's my son! *(Faints and falls to the ground)*

GIOVANNA: Look what you've done . . . blessed woman!

VERONICA: But I never thought it could have been his mother!

THE RESURRECTION OF LAZARUS

PROLOGUE

Now we come to the miracle of Lazarus.

This text is a "battle horse," demanding extraordinary physical and vocal agility, because the giullare finds himself playing the roles of something like fifteen or sixteen characters consecutively, indicating the changes with nothing but his body. He doesn't even alter his voice, but simply changes his attitude. Consequently this is one of the texts that forces the actor to improvise a little, adapting himself to the rhythm of the laughter, the tempo and the silences of the audience. Actually, it is a scenario that requires constant improvisation. The central theme of the text is found in its satire of everything that constitutes the "mystical moment," focusing on the exhibition of what people usually refer to as a "miracle." The satire is directed against the exhibition of the miraculous, of magic, of witchcraft, which is prevalent in many religions, including Catholicism, particularly the idea of exhibiting the miracle as a supernatural event, with the goal of demonstrating indisputably that it has been performed by God, whereas, in the original accounts of the miracle, it was interpreted as a sign of the love and connection that existed between the Divine and the human.

Here the miracle is recounted from the point of view of the faithful who come from the lower rungs of society. Everything is seen and presented as if it were a spectacle in which the "Divine Son of Man" exhibits himself as a great prestidigitator, a magician, someone who can do extraordinary things with great theatricality. There is no hint to the intentions behind the act.

In a sinopia from the cemetery in Pisa there is a depiction of the resurrection of Lazarus. (A sinopia is a preliminary sketch that precedes the execution of a fresco. During the restoration of this fresco, the well-preserved preliminary sketch had been uncovered.) Lazarus does not even appear in it: the attention is focused, as it will be in the piece that I am about to perform for you, on a crowd of astonished people, who express through gestures, their amazement at the miracle. One can also see a person in the crowd who takes advantage of the tension generated by the event. He slips his hand into the purse of a spectator, who is preoccupied with following the resurrection, and relieves him of a few coins.

———

The scene begins with conversation between the First Visitor and the Caretaker of the cemetery.

GIULLARE *(In the role of the First Visitor)*: Excuse me, is this the cemetery, the holy graveyard, where they're going to perform the resurrection of Lazarus, the one who was buried four days ago? And now a great holy man is coming, a witch doctor . . . I think his name is Jesus . . . "Son of God" is his nickname . . . and the corpse is going to jump up with his eyes rolling in his head and everyone will be shouting: "He's alive! He's alive!" And then we'll all go drinking and get divinely drunk. Is this the place?

(In the role of the Caretaker) Yes, two shekels if you want to see the miracle!

(As First Visitor) You want me to give you two shekels? Why?

(As Caretaker) Because I'm the caretaker of this cemetery and I've got to be compensated for all the trouble and damages you all are going to cause me . . . You people come in here and you stomp on the shrubbery . . . You trample all over the graves . . . you sit on the crosses . . . twist the arms off them . . . and then you even steal the candles! *(Takes a breath)* Two shekels, otherwise you can go to some other cemetery! I'd like to see if you can find

another holy man as good as ours, who with just a wave of his hands can bring the dead sprouting up out of the ground like mushrooms. Move along, move along! You too, lady, two shekels! Half a shekel for the baby. I don't care if he doesn't understand a thing. When he grows up you'll tell him: "What a shame you were too thick-headed and dumb to understand what was going on, and not only that, just at the moment of the miracle, you peed all over me!" *(He turns to an imaginary boy who's trying to sneak into the cemetery by climbing over the wall)* Get out of here! Off that wall! Troublemaker, riffraff! Wise guy . . . wants to come in and see the miracle for free.

(As First Visitor) Gosh, there's so many graves! What a big cemetery! Look at all the crosses. *(Turns directly to the audience)* I came here early on purpose to get a good place, because I like to be up front . . . I like to have a good view of the open grave . . . because some of these holy witch doctors will try to pull a fast one on you: they put a dead man on top, a live one underneath, they make all these holy gestures and—TRACHETE!—they pull the old switcheroo: "He's alive! He's alive!"

I want to see it up close! Last time I was here early in the morning, I spent half the day waiting around . . . but they performed the miracle over on the other side, so I ended up standing there like a dope without seeing a thing. But this time I'm going to get it right. And here is Lazarus! Look at all the people coming! *(Scans the people around him)* Hey! You like miracles, don't you? You don't have anything better to do, huh? *(Getting shoved and losing his equilibrium)* Stop pushing! We have an open grave here! I'll fall in, and then the holy man will come and say: "Alive! Alive!" And me, I'm already alive! *(Points into the distance)* They're even coming down from the mountains! . . . Hey, mountain boys, you never saw a miracle before, did you? *(Comments ironically)* Foreigners! *(Indicates the presence of a short man)* Hey, shorty, stop pushing! Shorty, stop pushing! I don't care if you're too short to see anything. Short people and cripples have to get here at dawn to find a good spot. *(Comments ironically)* Ha, ha, ha . . . you think you're in heaven where the little people will be first and the big people will be last? Ha, ha, ha! *(Turns to another spectator)* Oh, lady, don't push! I don't care if you're a woman. In the face of death, we're all equal!

(Directly to the audience) I don't just come here for the miracles. I come for the laughs. *(Shouting into the distance)* Well, is the holy man going to show up or what? Isn't there someone who knows where his house is who can go and call him . . . to let him know that we're all ready for him here . . . that we can't stand around all day waiting for miracles . . . We've got other things to do! . . . They should make a timetable for these miracles! And stick to it! *(To himself)* Is he coming? . . . *(To the others)* He's not coming!

(As a Man Renting Chairs, who is loudly offering his wares to the crowd) Chairs! Who wants chairs? Ladies! Rent yourself a chair! Two shekels a chair! Get yourself a seat, because it's very dangerous to watch a miracle while you're standing up. Because as soon as the holy man shows up and waves his arms, Lazarus is going to rise up onto his feet . . . with his eyes rolling in his head . . . and you'll be so terrified that you'll fall over backwards with a big thump and smash your head on a rock— TACCHETE!—stone cold dead! *(Turns to the audience)* And the holy man only performs one miracle a day! So step right up and rent a chair! Two shekels!

(As the First Visitor) Shorty, you got a chair, huh? To make yourself taller! Good for you! I'll help you climb up! Opla—now you're a big shorty! Don't lean on my shoulder . . . or I'll give you a good shove . . . knock you into the open tomb, grab the lid and slam it shut. *(Pretends to knock from the inside of the tomb)* TON-TON—silence! TON-TON—eternity! . . .

(Turns to those around him) Is this saint going to show up or isn't he? He's not coming! We can't keep waiting here like this . . . it's getting dark! We'll have to light little candles. The saint will get here, go to the wrong grave, and resurrect somebody else's corpse . . . Then Lazarus's

mother will show up, crying her eyes out . . . And we'll have to kill the corpse he just resurrected!

That wouldn't make a very nice impression . . . not in front of all the foreigners.

(As a Fried Fish Vendor) Ohhhhoooh! Sardines here! Nice sweet fried sardines . . . Two shekels . . . Get yourself a handful! So delicious . . . they bring the dead back to life!

(As First Visitor) Hey, sardine man, why don't you give a few to Lazarus to wake up his stomach!

(As Another Visitor) Be quiet! Blasphemer!

(As First Visitor) Look at all the people coming . . . look, look, all the apostles! They're lined up behind the holy man . . . that apostle over there . . . That's Peter, with the long beard and all the curls . . . and that other one with the bald head and the curly beard, that's Paul . . . And that one . . . *(Shouting out a festive greeting)* Maaaark! . . . *(Changing tone; turning proudly to the people around him)* I know him! He lives next door to my house . . . *(Waves his arms in a highly visible greeting, inviting the saint out for a drink after the miracle)* Look. That's Jesus . . . The little one . . . he's so young . . . Look, he doesn't even have a beard . . . he's so sweet . . . he looks like a little boy. I imagined him much heftier, with a huge head of hair . . . elephant ears *(Points to his ears)*, a giant coxcomb, tremendous teeth, and great big hands, so that when he makes the sign of the benediction—PAA!—he smacks the faithful to pieces! But he's so young! . . .

(The First Voice from the Crowd) Jeeesuuuus! Do that miracle again with the multiplication of the bread and the fishes that was so delicious . . . God, what a feast that was!

(Another Voice from the Crowd) Don't you ever think of anything but food!?

(The First Voice from the Crowd) It's natural! Here we are standing around the cemetery . . . and the excitement of waiting for the miracle gets my stomach so worked-up that I'm hungry enough to eat God himself!

(Another Visitor) Quiet, quiet! Jesus just gave the word for everybody to get down on their knees! All the holy

men are on their knees praying . . . so are the others . . .
We should get down on our knees, too, otherwise the miracle won't work!

(And Another Visitor) I won't do it. I won't do it! I don't
care! I'm not a believer and I'm not getting down on my
knees!

(Yet Another Visitor) May you be hit with a lightning
bolt that will cripple your leg. *(Walks with a limp)* Then
you'll go to Jesus: "Jesus, can you do that miracle for me,
the one . . ." Nothing doing! Another lightning bolt—
TRAK!—there go your arms too! *(Mimics paralyzed arms)*

(And Another Visitor) Quiet, quiet, he's given the order
to lift the stone off the grave. *(A bystander shouts orders
and supervises the raising of the stone)* Come on! All
together! Lift that boulder! Watch out for your toes!

(And Another Visitor holds his nose) Wooah—what a
stench! That stinks! What do they have in there—a putrefied cat?

(And Another . . .) No, no, it's him, it's Lazarus, look
what a state he's in!

(And Another . . .) Ohia—he's almost rotted away—
all those worms are coming out of his eyes! Ah, that's
disgusting!

(And Another . . .) What a joke they're playing on him!

(And Another . . .) On who?

(And Another . . .) On him, on Jesus! They told him the
guy had only been buried four days . . . but it looks like
he's been down under for at least a month! He'll never
pull off this miracle . . .

(And Another . . .) Why?

(And Another . . .) Because this corpse is too ripe.

(And Another . . .) I think he'll do it anyway, because
this holy man is so great that even if there were nothing
left in the grave but four putrid decomposing bones, all
he'd have to do was lift his eyes up to heaven . . . Two
words to his father, and before you know it those bones
would be full of flesh and muscles and—VUUUUUUMM-
MMM!—he'd jump right up out of there like a rabbit!

(And Another . . .) Cut the crap!

(And Another . . .) What crap?! Why don't we bet on it? Four will get you five if he pulls it off!

(Yet Another . . .) Seven will get you ten if he can't do it! I'm taking all bets! *(Turns to the other spectators with the tone of a bookmaker taking odds)* Three, four, two . . . eight says he can do it . . . seven says he can't . . .

(And Another . . .) Stop it! Shame on you! The holy man's still praying, and they're taking bets! Blasphemy! You should be ashamed of yourselves . . . *(Suddenly)* I bet you five shekels he can do it!

(And Another . . .) Quiet! The holy man pointed to the corpse and commanded: "Rise up, Lazarus!"

(And Another . . .) Ha, ha! All that's going to rise up are the worms crawling around in his belly.

(Another . . .) Quiet, you blasphemer!

(Another . . . dumbfounded) He's moving! God bless him, he's moving! He's alive! *(Acts out the movement of Lazarus, who rises up, wobbling)* Lazarus sits up, rises, he's on his feet! He's falling, falling, falling . . . He's going down, he's going down! He's coming up! He's shaking himself off like a wet dog shaking off water . . . Worms are flying all over the place! *(Disgust as he cleans off the worms that have been shaken onto his face and body)* Miserable wretch! Take it easy with those worms!

(Another . . . falling onto his knees) It's a miracle! He's alive! He's been resurrected! Woooah, look at that—he's laughing, he's crying. *(In turn each Visitor marvels at the miracle)*

(And Another Visitor, also dropping to his knees) Amazing Son of God, I had no idea you were this miraculous! *(Turns quickly to the bookmaker)* I won. You owe me seven shekels! *(To Jesus)* It's amazing! Bravo, Jesus, bravo! . . . *(Pats his belly and his hips)* My purse? . . . Thief! Bravo, Jesus! *(Turns toward the distance)* Thief! Thief! Jesus, bravo! *(Exits running, repeatedly turning his head back and forth between Jesus and the imaginary thief he is pursuing in the distance)* Thieeeeef! . . . Jesus! Bravo, Jesus! Thieeef! Bravo, Jesus! Thieeef! Bravooooooo, Jesus!

THE MIRACLE OF
THE WEDDING AT CANA

An Englishman by the name of Smith who lived in the nineteenth century collected in one volume numerous sacred representations from Italy. *(A slide is projected)* Look, this is a slide of a mystery play that is still performed today in Sicily, in the area known as "la Piana dei Greci" ("the Plain of the Greeks"). This choral action shows three different rituals being played out through the enactment of a single analogous situation: the entrance of Christ into Jerusalem hailed as the king of Israel, accompanied by celebrants waving olive branches and palm fronds; it also represents Bacchus, the god of happiness and inebriation, in procession with his satyrs; and finally Dionysus, accompanied by the bacchants and the followers of Silenus, descends to the underworld. In regards to this divinity of the early Greeks, whose origins go back to Thessaly and Minoa, we have to remember that in the first Christian catacombs we find the figure of Christ represented with the same images used for the ancient Greek gods. About him it is told that when Pluto, god of darkness, came up to the Earth to kidnap Persephone, virgin goddess of "the new April" (as they sing in a Tuscan homage), to drag her down to the underworld to enjoy her all for himself, Dionysus, moved by his great love for the human race, sacrifices himself. He gets on the back of a mule, goes down to Hades, and pays the price of his own life to restore to mankind the sweet young girl, the symbol of springtime.

105

Jesus also, we are taught, is a god who arrives on Earth to try to give springtime back to mankind.

This merging of the divinities and their stories into one another, we should note, does not occur by chance in the history of world religions, but instead resembles a design of concentric circles in which each reproduces the same motif, transforming it and retelling it ad infinitum. In recounting the mystery play called "The Miracle of the Wedding at Cana," which is both sacred and comic at the same time, we have the character of the drunkard, the guiding spirit of the tale, who tells how he found himself at a wedding feast, where he got drunk on homemade wine created there on the spot by Jesus Christ. Jesus Christ, as it turns out, becomes Bacchus, and at a certain point is represented standing on a table, in a state of exaltation, urging all the wedding guests: "Drink up, people. Be happy. That's what counts. Don't wait for Paradise later. Paradise is also here on Earth."

This is exactly the opposite of what is taught to us in the religious doctrines from the time we are children, when they tell us that we have to put up with things: We're in a valley of tears . . . Not everyone can be rich . . . Some do well, some do poorly, but everyone will get what they deserve when we get to the next world . . . Don't worry, be good, and don't break our balls. That's what it comes down to, more or less.

There are two characters at the heart of this performance: the drunkard and the angel. The angel (or rather the archangel) would like to present the prologue of a sacred spectacle, as it is told in the traditional canon. The loquacious drunkard, however, wants at any cost to tell the story as he experienced it in person, to bear witness to how smashing it was to get plastered on the wine at the wedding in Cana.

The angel speaks in an aristocratic dialect from Venice, elegant, foreboding. The drunkard uses a crude vernacular, boorish and highly colorful.

The two get into a spat that degenerates into kicks and blows, and the angel is forced to flee.

I will perform the tale without the assistance of a supporting actor, not through any excess of exhibitionism, but because the piece imposes on me the structure of a monologue. We have tried many times to put a scene of this type on the stage with several actors, but we discovered that it doesn't function. When presented in the form of a dialogue, the action stagnates, resulting in a rhythm plagued by dead spots that deflate all the comic and dramatic tension.

On the other hand, the storytelling technique of the giullare, a solo performer, utilizes the effects of synthesis and doubles the speed, projecting a tightly played sequence of suggestive actions, charged with imaginative theatricality that doubles both the tension and the comedy.

So, when I'm on this side of the stage *(Points to his left)* I'll be playing the part of the angel—aristocratic, with refined gestures. When I move to the other side *(Points to the right)* I'll be the drunkard. While the character of the angel remains onstage, a slide will be projected on the backdrop (an "Angel" by Cimabue, at Assisi, in the triforium of Saint Francis, from the end of the thirteenth century).

———

The Angel turns to his public, lifting his arms in the manner of a great orator.

ANGEL: Pay attention, good people, because I want to speak to you of a true story, a story that began—

DRUNKARD *(Interrupting)*: I also want to tell you a marvelous story . . . of the most wonderful drinking binge I've ever had!

ANGEL: Be quiet, you big lush!

DRUNKARD: I want to talk, too . . .

ANGEL: No! You're not talking! I am the prologue and I'm delivering the prologue by myself! Get out!

DRUNKARD *(Tries to speak)*: But . . .

ANGEL: Silence! You drunkard!

DRUNKARD: Can't I even tell them about—

ANGEL: No!

DRUNKARD: Eh . . . but I . . .

ANGEL: No, you're not saying a word! Shhhhh! . . . *(Back to the public)* Good people . . . Everything that I'm about to tell you is completely true. It is all taken from the Gospels. What little we have added by way of the imagination . . .

DRUNKARD *(Whispering)*: Later *(Gesturing with his finger)* I'll tell you about that wonderful drinking binge—

ANGEL: Oh! Drunkard!

DRUNKARD: I didn't do anything . . . It was just my finger . . .

ANGEL: Not even a finger!

DRUNKARD: But I don't make any noise with my finger!

ANGEL: Yes, you're making noise . . . You're going: "Rrrrrrr!"

DRUNKARD: It's not true!

ANGEL: Silence!

DRUNKARD: Am I allowed to breathe at least?

ANGEL: No!

DRUNKARD: I can't breathe?

ANGEL: No!

DRUNKARD: Not even through my nose? . . .

ANGEL: No!

DRUNKARD: If I don't breathe, I'll explode!

ANGEL: Explode!

DRUNKARD: Ah, but . . . if I explode, I'll make noise, eh!

ANGEL: Explode in silence!

DRUNKARD: Oh, but it's difficult to explode in silence!

ANGEL: Silence!

DRUNKARD *(Tries to speak again)*: But I can't—

ANGEL *(Interrupting him)*: Siiiiiiilence! *(To the audience)* Everything that I am about to tell you is completely true, it is all taken from the books of the Gospels . . . The few things that we have added by way of the imagination . . .

(The Drunkard comes up behind the Angel's back and plucks out one of his feathers.)

DRUNKARD *(In a low voice, to himself)*: Oh, what a pretty colored feather . . .

ANGEL: Drunkard! . . .

(The Drunkard stops in fear, throws the feather into the air and mimes its trajectory as it floats down into his mouth. He coughs loudly.)

DRUNKARD: Eh . . . But . . . You made me swallow it! *(Twists his torso as if his stomach is being tickled from the inside)* It tickles!

ANGEL *(Contemptuous)*: Silence!

DRUNKARD: Eh, but I . . . can't . . .

ANGEL: Get out!

DRUNKARD: But I . . . *(Continues to snicker from the tickling)* Oh, oh . . .

ANGEL *(Casts a glance at the Drunkard and continues his speech)*: Everything that I am about to tell you is completely true, everything is taken from books, from the Gospels . . .

(The Drunkard turns toward the Angel and plucks another feather out from behind him. He admires it. He plucks out another and sniffs it. Disgusted, he tosses it away. Using the feather as a fan, he cools himself off. The Angel notices.)

Drunkard! . . .

DRUNKARD: Eh? . . . *(Throws the feather in the air and mimes it coming down again like snow)* It's snowing . . .

ANGEL: Would you like to get off this stage? If you don't get off it soon, I'm going to throw you off it with a big kick!

DRUNKARD: A kick?

ANGEL: Yes, a kick! Get out!

DRUNKARD *(To the audience, indignant)*: People! Did you hear that? An angel who wants to throw me out with a kick . . . to kick me! An angel!

(Aggressively to the Angel) Come here, come here, angel face, come here you oversized rooster! I'm going to pluck your feathers one by one, out of your ass too . . . *(Moves closer; menacingly)* Straight from your butt . . . come here, you big chicken . . . Come here!

ANGEL: Help . . . Don't touch me! Help! Murderer! *(Runs away in terror)*

DRUNKARD: The angel ran away and called me a murderer! But how could he call me a murderer? How could he call someone a murderer who is so full of goodwill. I'm so good that goodness has been coming out of my ears thanks to that wine that's swishing all over the place, overflowing onto the ground so you can slosh around in it. I couldn't have imagined that this day would end so nicely, since it started out so miserable. Dammit . . . I was invited to a wedding, a spousing, in a place nearby called Cana . . . Cana . . . and that's why from now on they'll call it "The Wedding at Cana." Okay, so I went! I get there . . . and there's a big table full of stuff to eat. Lots of guests . . . not sitting, everybody's standing up, either cursing or spitting on the ground or kicking the stones so hard it made them spin.

The bride was crying. The mother of the bride was pulling her hair out. The father of the bride was in front of a wall banging his head into it over and over again. It was an ugly scene!

"But what happened?" I asked.

"Oh, what a disaster!"

"Did the groom run away?"

"No, the groom is over there," *(Pointing)* "cursing more than anyone!"

"So what happened?"

"What a disaster . . . we discovered that a vat full of wine prepared for the wedding banquet has turned to vinegar!"

"All to vinegar? Dammit, what a disaster! A wet bride is a lucky bride, but getting soaked with vinegar is bad luck that needs to be squelched and belched away."

And everybody was crying. The groom was cursing, the mother of the bride was tearing out her hair, the bride was crying, the father of the bride was in front of a wall banging his head into it over and over again. It was an ugly scene!

Meanwhile a young kid shows up, by the name of Jesus . . . I think his last name was Son of God. He wasn't alone. No, he was accompanied by his mamma, who everybody called Madonna. *(Suggests an elegant and fascinating way of walking)* Very refined lady! They were important guests who were arriving fashionably late. As soon as this lady Madonna figured out what was going on, what with the wine turning to vinegar and everything, she went up to Jesus, Son of God, and also of the Madonna, and told him, *(Speaking the words very rapidly, one after the other, without taking a breath)* "You, my son who is such a dear kind boy, who is always doing miraculous things for everyone who needs them, in this moment of sadness, see what you can do to get these poor people out of this embarrassing mess and give them something to be happy about, and remember with pleasure on this holy day. Hallelujah! Hallelujah!"

As soon as the Madonna had had this little chat with her son, we saw blossoming on the lips of Jesus a smile so sweet, so very sweet . . . that if you weren't careful, you would be so moved by it that your kneecaps would fall off onto your big toes. And all of a sudden this Jesus said: "All right, people, can I have twelve pitchers full of clear clean water?"

There was a lightning bolt—TRACH!—twelve pitchers appeared there in front of him, full of water, so that I, not used to seeing so much water at once, started feeling a little ill . . . it felt like I was drowning . . . Dammit!

It was as quiet as a church service, and this Jesus massaged his hands, rubbing them together and cracking his knuckles. *(Illustrates, pulling his fingers)* And then he raised three fingers—only three fingers, the other two he kept pressed against his palm—and he began to make signs over the water . . . signs that only the Son of God can make. Me, I was already a little under the weather (like I said, looking at water makes me queasy), I didn't look . . . I stared out sadly into the distance . . . and suddenly my nostrils were filled with the aroma of crushed grapes. There was no mistake about it. It was wine! Dammit, what a wine! They passed me a goblet, I pressed my lips against it, I sucked down a drop . . . *(As if in ecstasy)* Dammit! . . . Oh . . . Oh . . . bless the souls in purgatory, what a wine! . . . Slightly mellow, bitterish at the bottom, a little bubbly, salted in the middle, so it had a magenta glow all through it, without mustiness or froth, aged just about three seasons . . . it was a very good year! It slid so smoothly down your throat and gurgled in your stomach . . . then it spread out just a little with a quiver, resting there calmly, as if to catch its breath, then—GNOCK!—it gives you a hit, turns around back up your throat, making its way all the way to your nostrils, and releasing such a strong aroma . . . that even a man riding by on horse-back— *(Mimes a horse rearing up to jump, and a dumb-founded rider in a monumental pose)* GNIUU . . . BLLL— would smell it and shout: "It's springtime!"

What a wine! And everyone was applauding: "Bravo, Jesus. De wine is de-vine!" And everybody was guzzling it down, getting pickled, dancing. The bride danced, the groom sang. The father of the bride was still in front of the wall smashing his head into it over and over again. What a shame, nobody told him about the miracle!

Jesus stood up on a table and poured out wine for everyone: "Drink, people, make merry, be happy! Drink yourselves silly, don't wait until later . . . Heaven is here, enjoy it now . . . not after you die!"

Suddenly he remembered that his mother was there: "Excuse me, Mamma, my thoughts are getting a little muddled . . . Drink a drop of wine, Mamma!"

"No, no, son, thank you. I thank you, but I can't drink, because I'm not used to wine . . . it makes my head spin . . . and then I say silly things."

"But no, Mamma, it won't do you any harm, it will just bring you a little happiness! It can't hurt you. This wine is good and healthy and pure . . . I made it myself."

(To the audience, changing tone and attitude) And then there are still lousy skunks running around saying that wine is an invention of the satanic devil . . . but do you think that if wine had been a demonic and sinful creation that Jesus would have given it to his mother to drink? To his own mother? Why he has more love for her than I have for all the grappa in the world! I am sure that if God the Father in person, instead of waiting all that time to teach Noah that wonderful trick of crushing grapes to extract wine, had taught Adam how to do it right from the start, *(Raising his voice)* immediately, before Eve, immediately, when he shaped him out of the mud, *(Mimes the action of a sculptor creating a puppet from clay)* like he was making gnocchi from the dough . . . *(Alludes to the head of the puppet)* He made two holes for the eyes, then inside the eye holes, those round little meatballs . . . two scoops for

the ears, the nose with holes, the mouth . . . *(Pretends to put two fingers inside the puppet's mouth)* Careful not to bite with those little teeth, eh! Then the neck . . . the shoulders, the elbows, the fingers . . . I'll make them like mine . . . *(Counts his own fingers)* One, two, three, four, five on each side . . . then under the belly, your equipment, *(Mimes with discretion the placement of Adam's sex)* the little birdie, the little cheeks, down to the legs, the feet— here too, five toes . . . Now I'll give you life— *(As if breathing into his mouth)* FFFPPPHHOO—breathe, Adam! *(Breathes like a bellows and compels him to take in the air by force)* Ah, ah, ah, ah . . . open your eyes . . . go, Adam, now that you have life! *(Holds up the creature while trying to make him walk)* Now I'm going to make you a vat. *(Makes the gestures of shaping a huge vat and inviting Adam to step into it)* Get in, get into the vat . . . now the grapes, look, what a cluster of grapes . . . go on, crush the grapes, go on, dance on them, that's it . . . *(Incites him to dance and to stamp on the must, clapping his hands to mark the rhythm)*

(Detaching himself from the action, he steps to the edge of the stage and comments heatedly) That's it! That's it! God should have taught them right away: "Adam, grape, wine, Eve!" Then we wouldn't be in this accursed world. We'd all be in heaven. *(Gestures raising a glass for a toast)* To your health! Because all it would have taken on that accursed day when the sneaky snake with the apple in his mouth came up to Adam and said *(In the tone of a huckster)*: "Eat the apple, Adam!" *(As if miming an Oriental dance with the twisting movements of the snake wrapping itself around Adam while holding the apple in its open jaws)* "Sweet, delicious, sweet apple, red, delicious apple, like a grape!" All it would have taken would have been for Adam to have hidden behind his back a big glass full of wine . . . he would have kicked the apple to the ground, trampled on the head of the snake and shouted *(Making a toast)*: "To your health! That's it! To you, to him, happiness, with God, to the Earth!"

THE WEDDING AT CANA

113

FOOL'S PLAY UNDER THE CROSS

THE CRUCIFIERS ("THE NAILERS")

PROLOGUE

In Umbria the term "nailer" refers to the man who nails Christ to the cross during the performances of the lauds. In the Po valley they use the term "spiker" or "crucifier." In the passion play performed in the dialect of that region, which we will now present for you, there are four or more "nailers" directed by their supervisor.

This year in Pisa you can see an exhibition of statues from the twelfth and thirteenth centuries depicting life-size saints reacting around the cross. Originally these painted statues were used in the passion plays: the crucified Christ was represented with articulated arms, wrist, bust and legs, so that the descent from the cross could be done in a way that made Jesus seem real.

The crucifixion that we are presenting for you now is certainly from that period. The technique used by the four nailers to stretch out and hoist Jesus onto the cross is described with surprising, almost obsessive, precision. One gets the impression that in those times the act of nailing people on crosses was very well known and even fashionable. On the other hand, we know that this horrendous form of execution continued to be practiced until the eighth and ninth centuries. This is the reason why up to that day, in the frescoes and miniatures that depict the life of Christ, the moment of the crucifixion is inevitably censored—one cannot be permitted to get down on one's knees and pray to a man (even if he's Divine) condemned to the cross, and then leave the church to find a real one hoisted up on an analogous crucifix.

—

VERSION FOR MULTIPLE GIULLARI

Five men (the Nailers), with mallets and long nails strapped to their belts, stand ready to crucify Christ. The cross is already laid out on the ground. In the background, behind a stretched-out sheet, we see the silhouette of Jesus, who, constrained by soldiers, undresses, while some women off to the side follow the action. Standing on a stool is the Clown Auctioneer.

CLOWN: Women! You women enamored of Christ, come feast your eyes . . . come see the lovely nude man undress himself, your beloved . . . two bits for a peep, come women! What a beautiful thing to purchase! They say he was the Son of God: to me it seems he is equal to another man . . . equal in every way! Two bits to look at him, ladies! Doesn't anyone want to purge their sins for two bits? *(No reaction on the part of the women)* All right, today's a holiday . . . I'm going to make an offer that will ruin me . . . *(Turns to a woman)* Come here, you. I'm going to let you take a look for free . . . *(The woman does not move)* Oh, what a fusspot . . . come here! Don't miss the opportunity . . . *(Looks at her more carefully)* It's not you, Mary Magdalene, who loved him so much that when you couldn't find a napkin or towel to dry his feet, dried them with your own hair? *(Receives no response)* All right, it's your loss . . . because now, as the law demands, we have to cover him up, and hide his sin . . . with a little smock like the ones the ballerinas use! *(Speaks to someone offstage)* Is the head comedian ready? Pull back the curtain and let's start the show! *(The curtain is raised, revealing Christ behind it)* First Scene: The Son of God, great horseman with a crown, mounts his steed . . . a great big wooden horse, to go jousting. And to be sure he doesn't fall to the ground—we're going to nail him to the saddle by his hands and feet!

(Christ is stretched out on the cross.)

HEAD NAILER: Stop playing the clown and come here and give us a hand . . . Tie a rope to his wrists, one on each side, so he gets stretched out nice and long . . . leave his palms free so we can pound the nails in. I'll hammer this one on the right, and . . .

FIRST NAILER: And I'll get this other one. Throw me over a long nail. I've got my hammer. Oh, what a big nail! What do you bet I can hammer the whole thing through with seven whacks?

SECOND NAILER: And what will you bet me that I can do mine in six?

HEAD NAILER: Okay. Come on, get going you two. We have to put wings on this little angel so he can fly in the sky like Icarus. *(Pause)* Let's pull together . . . I said together! . . . You pulled him out of line! Slowly—so we can put this horseman in the middle of the saddle . . . A little more towards me . . . good, I'm on the mark . . . right in the hole. *(Points to a hole that has already been prepared in the board)*

SECOND NAILER: I'm not there yet. You made the holes too far apart! You pull harder! Did you eat too much cheese for lunch? Harder!

FIRST NAILER: Yes, harder! We're going to end up ripping the ligaments of his shoulders and elbows.

HEAD NAILER: Don't worry, they're not your ligaments! Pull! Eh, eh, harder!

(The groans of Christ are amplified in counterpoint by the lamentations of the women.)

FIRST NAILER: Did you hear that crack?

SECOND NAILER: Yes, it wasn't pretty . . . it was a shock that snapped the bones . . . Now he's stretched out according to the measurements—now I'm over the hole too.

HEAD NAILER: Good. *(Turning to the other soldiers)* You hold the ropes taut . . . and you lift your hammer so we can start together.

SECOND NAILER: Be careful not to hit your fingers!

(General snickering.)

FIRST NAILER *(To Christ)*: Stretch out this paw so I don't tickle you! . . . Oh, look at the lifeline he's got on this hand! The line is so long it looks like he's destined to survive at least another fifty years, this horseman! Go ahead and believe those fairy tales the witches tell you!

SECOND NAILER: Stop blabbing and lift your hammer.

FIRST NAILER: I'm ready.

HEAD NAILER: Hit it now . . . *(Raising his voice, he gives the order)* Hammer the first blow . . . *(A thump)* Ohioa-ahhh!

(Christ shouts.)

CLOWN: They nailed his palms!

HEAD NAILER *(In counterpoint to the shouts of Christ)*: Ohooo, he's shaking all over. Calm down! *(Giving the order)* Hammer the second blow!

CHRIST: Ohaoioaohh!

HEAD NAILER: To stretch out the bones.

CHRIST: Ohoh!

HEAD NAILER: Spit blood on the knuckles. Hammer the third blow!

CHRIST: Ohahiohoh!

HEAD NAILER: This nail has deflowered you . . .

CHRIST: Ohoh!

HEAD NAILER: . . . since no woman ever overpowered you. The soldiers will give you the gift of a fourth blow!

CHRIST: Ohahiohoh!

HEAD NAILER: Since you said that no man should kill another!

CHRIST: Ohahiohoh!

HEAD NAILER: And all men should love their enemies like a brother! The fifth blow will be delivered by the bishops of the synagogue!

CHRIST: Ohahiohoh!

HEAD NAILER: Since you said that they were evil and dishonest!

CHRIST: Ohahiohoh!

HEAD NAILER: That your bishops will all be humble and impoverished. The gift of the sixth blow will be delivered by the rich men!

CHRIST: Ohahiohoh!

HEAD NAILER: Whom you said won't get to heaven no matter how hard they try!

CHRIST: Ohahiohoh!

HEAD NAILER: When you gave the example of the camel in the needle's eye. The seventh blow will be struck by the imposters!

CHRIST: Ohahioh!

HEAD NAILER: Whose prayers you discounted as worthless.

CHRIST: Ohahiohoh!

HEAD NAILER: That they could cheat all the assholes on Earth, but the Lord was not one to mess with.

FIRST NAILER: I won! You owe me a drink, and don't forget it.

CLOWN: Let's drink to the health of this horseman and to his misfortune! *(To Christ)* How are things going, Your Majesty? Does he feel firmly in your grip, this war horse? Good— now we'll go jousting, without a spear or shield!

HEAD NAILER: Did you untie the cord from his wrists? Good work, my barons . . . pull the wrapping tight around his shoulders, so he doesn't fall down when we lift him up, this champion! As soon as we nail in his feet, we can take it off . . .

(The Nailers wrap up Christ's chest so that it is attached to the cross.)

SECOND NAILER: Come here everyone . . . spit on your hands and let's hoist up this greased pole! You come up front with the ropes and loop them over the transverse plank . . . you too, Fool, climb up to the top of the ladder, and get ready to grab it.

FOOL: I'm sorry, but I can't help you; that man never did anything to me . . .

SECOND NAILER: What a dope! He didn't do anything to us either. We're just crucifying him to pass the time! *(Laughs sneeringly)* Ha, ha . . . and they gave us ten bits a head for our trouble! Come on, give us a hand, and then afterwards we'll give you the honor of playing a round of dice with us . . .

FOOL: That's great . . . if it's a round that doesn't set me back too much! I'm already on the ladder, look . . . you can get started!

HEAD NAILER: Good work! Is everybody ready? Let's go then, pull together . . . pay attention, one long pull at a time. I'll keep the beat.

Oh, we're hoisting	Ehie
The mast of this ship	Ohoho
And as our flag	Ohoho
We've put a fool on top	Ohoho
Oh, we're hoisting	Ehiee
This festival maypole	Ohoho
This thick, greased pole	Ohoho
With Jesus Christ at the foretop	Ohoho
Oh, what a greased pole	Ahaaa
Making a hole in the sky	Ohoho
That rains down blood on us	Ohoho
Rejoice, rejoice	Ehiee
For we've found the one who was brave	Ohoho
Who made himself a slave	Ohoho
And all souls he will save.	Ohoho.

(In the manner of a horseman) Whoooaaa . . . that's enough! *(The cross has been raised)* It looks nice and sturdy. Good . . . *(To the Fool)* Now, take out the dice and we'll play.

(The players quickly mime a variety of dice and tarot card games. The Fool wins the shroud of Christ and the pay of the Nailers.)

FOOL: If you want your money back, I'll give it to you gladly . . . including the necklace, the earrings, the ring . . . and look, I'll throw this in too! *(Adds a bracelet)*

FIRST NAILER: And what do you want in exchange for all this stuff?

FOOL: That one there . . . *(Points to Christ)*

SECOND NAILER: Christ?

FOOL: Yes, I want you to let me take him down from the cross.

HEAD NAILER: Fine! Wait until he dies and he's yours!

FOOL: No, I want him now while he's still alive.

FIRST NAILER: Oh, fool of all fools, do you want all four of us to end up nailed in his place?

FOOL: No, don't worry. Nothing will happen to you. All we have to do is put up someone else in his place, somebody his size, and you'll see that no one will notice the switch . . . because up on a cross everybody looks alike.

FIRST NAILER: That's true . . . flayed out like that, he looks like a fish on a grill . . .

HEAD NAILER: It may be true, but I don't like the idea. And besides, who do you have in mind to put in his place?

FOOL: Judas!

HEAD NAILER: Judas? That one . . .

FOOL: Yes, the traitorous apostle who hung himself out of desperation from the fig tree behind the hedge, fifty steps from here.

HEAD NAILER: Get moving, hurry . . . let's go and strip him to see if his purse is still filled with the thirty coins he got for his trouble.

FOOL: No, don't bother . . . he threw them out right away, into the middle of a patch of thorns.

HEAD NAILER: How do you know?

FOOL: I know because I picked up the money myself . . . one coin at a time. You can see the scratches on my arms.

HEAD NAILER: I'm not interested in your arms . . . show us the money.

(The Fool shows them the money.)

Ohi, ohi—they're all silver. Look how pretty they are . . . how heavy . . . how they sound!

FOOL: Good, take them. They're yours too if you agree to my trade. As for me . . . I agree.

HEAD NAILER: So do we.

FOOL: Good, so go quickly and get the hanged Judas, and I'll take care of getting Christ down.

FIRST NAILER: And what if the centurions show up and catch you red-handed?

FOOL: I'll tell them it was my idea . . . after all, I'm a fool . . . and you won't be held responsible in any way. But don't stand there wasting time. Get moving!

HEAD NAILER: Yes, yes, let's go . . . and let's hope they don't bring us bad luck, these thirty coins.

(The Nailers and soldiers exit.)

FOOL: Good, it's done. It doesn't seem real to me! I'm so happy! Jesus, be strong, your salvation has arrived . . . I've got the pincers . . . here they are . . . You never would have thought, Jesus, that you would end up being saved by a fool . . . Ha, ha . . . wait, first I'll support you with this strap, it will only take a minute . . . Don't worry, I won't hurt you . . . I'll get you down as gently as a bride and then I'll carry you over my shoulders, because I'm as strong as an ox . . . and then we'll take off! I'll bring you down to the river where I have a little boat and with four strokes we'll get to the other side . . . And quick as a wink we'll find ourselves glowing like the sun at the house of a friend of mine who's a shaman, and he'll give you some medicine and have you all healed up in three days. *(Pause)* You don't want to? You don't want the shaman? Fine, we'll go to the herbal doctor, who's also a very good friend of mine. *(Pause)* Not him either? What do you want then? *(Pause)* Nothing . . . you don't want me to un-nail you? I understand . . . you're convinced that with these holes in your hands and feet, the way they tore up all your ligaments, you won't be able to get around any-more, or eat on your own. *(Pause)* You don't want to stay in the world if you have to be dependent on others like a miserable wretch . . . did I guess it? *(Pause)* No, it's not that either? Oh, dammit! Then what's the reason? *(Pause)* For the sacrifice? What are you talking about? The salva-tion . . . . The redemption . . . You're not making sense! Oh, poor man . . . I bet . . . you've got a fever . . . feel how you're burning! Fine, but now I'm going to take you down and cover you up all cozy in your shroud . . . Excuse me for saying so, but you're as stubborn as a mule! *(Pause)* You don't want to be saved? You want to die here on these beams? *(Pause)* Yes? For the salvation of mankind . . . Oh, this is unbelievable! . . . And they call me a fool, but you've got me beaten by a mile, my dear son Jesus! And after I killed myself playing cards all night, this is the fine satisfaction that I get! Well, holy moly, you're the Son of God, aren't you? That much I know . . . Correct me if I'm wrong, so, since you are God, you know very well what will come of your sacrifice of dying on the cross . . . I'm not God, and I'm no prophet either, but last night a pale lady told me, through her tears, how it would all turn out. First, you'll be turned into gold, all gold, from your head down to your feet. Then they'll turn these iron nails into silver, and your tears will become sparkling pieces of diamonds. They'll turn all these drops of your blood into a stream of sparkling rubies. And all of this from you—who talked yourself hoarse—to speak to them of poverty.

And on top of that, they'll plant this cross of yours everywhere: on shields, on war banners, on swords that butcher people as if they were sheep. They'll even kill in your name—you who shouted that we are all brothers, that we should not kill. *(Pause)* You've already had a Judas . . . Well, you will have Judases swarming all over like ants, betraying you, using you to beat the shit out of each other! Believe me, it's not worth the trouble . . . *(Pause)* Eh? They won't all be traitors? All right, give me some names . . . The blessed Francis . . . and then Nicolas . . . Saint Martin of the cloak . . . Domenico . . . Catherine and Chiara . . . and then—okay, I'll give you those, but there will only be four good souls compared to all the miscreants . . . and even those four good souls will find themselves going through the same things that happened to you, after they've been crushed alive. *(Pause)* Say that again, please, because I didn't understand. *(Pause)* Even if there were only one . . . yes, even just one man in all the world worthy of being saved because he was honest, your sacrifice would not be in vain . . . Oh no, no . . . now

there's no hope left . . . you really are the king of the fools
. . . you're a one-man madhouse!

The only time you made me happy, Jesus, was when
you went into the church that they were turning into a
marketplace and you began to beat them all—the thieves,
the schemers, the imposters, the charlatans—all of them
with a big stick. Oh, what a beautiful sight! That was your
calling . . . You should beat them and thrash them! Give
them a good beating, a thrashing.

VERSION FOR SOLO GIULLARE

PROLOGUE

What follows is the same piece about the drama under the cross,
but now presented by the fool as the absolute protagonist. In this
version we find another text that requires the presence of a solo
performer acting out all the roles (except Christ): from the group
of nailers to the fool himself. The figure of Christ is created with a
polychrome wooden statue which has moving parts (as in the
multicharacter version above). It is identical to those used in the
Tuscan and Umbrian mystery plays from the tenth to the thirteenth centuries, of which several examples are extant.

—

*The Giullare, in the clothes of the Fool, is squatting. He mimes a
card game.*

FOOL *(Slapping cards on a table)*: King, goblets, woman on a
horse! I lost! *(Taking cards dealt by one of the players)* The
wagon, two brothers, five of staffs, and I finish with the
emperor. I lost again! I'm paying, I'm paying. Take your
money! Here it is! I haven't won a thing. *(Getting to his feet
and moving toward Christ on the cross. To his fellow players)* Excuse me . . . no, no, stay there . . . wait for me . . .
I'll be right back! *(Raises his gaze upward, speaking to
Christ on the cross)* Jesus, I'm sorry, but I've got a few bones

to pick with you . . . I know it's not good manners to go around busting the blessed balls of somebody who's already suffering on the cross . . . nailed to it even! But I've come to ask if you could do me a favor—Jesus, I'm someone who has never won a game, not a single round . . . because I'm always surrounded by these miscreant charlatans who cheat at the game like junk dealers selling gold-covered lead. They don't play fair with the cards . . . you know it, you see it, you do see it . . . *(Calling out to Christ, whose head was looking the other way)* Jesus, I'm here . . . where are you looking?! *(With difficulty, Christ turns his head toward him. [It is known that all the stage statues can be moved by means of strings activated from the wings or from overhead.] With the tone and gestures of a supplicant)* Jesus, be good, be kind to me, give me the wondrous pleasure of letting me win at least once. *(Taps lightly on the pole of the cross as if to spur Christ on)* Jesus, give me a sign! Oh yes, all right, it's a little difficult to do with your hands nailed down . . . *(Changes tone)* With your eyes . . . blink your eyes. Did you blink? Do it again. *(Exultant)* You blinked! You blinked! Oh, my dear man! I could come up there and hug you! You're really going to make me win, eh . . . don't joke around with me, or I'll blaspheme against you . . . Swear on your father that you told me so! You know it would be a lousy thing to do, for somebody up on the cross to play a trick on me just before dropping dead . . . It would be a bad joke! All right . . . I'm going to play, Jesus.

(To the other card players) Listen up . . . I'm coming back to the game! Get ready! *(Almost in gibberish, he goes on, as in the beginning, indicating the sign of each card as he throws it on the table)* The soldier with the joker, the horse over the queen—it's mine! *(Collecting his winnings)* You have the moon, he's got the sorceress, I have the devil—it's mine! *(Turns to Christ)* Dammit, Jesus, you've got the power! *(Continues the game)* Let's start again. King of staffs, the virgin with the goat, earthquake with the fathead—it's mine! *(Turning again to Christ)* You're overdoing it! Five in a row!

(To the other card players) Aren't you playing anymore? Don't you have any more money? I'll give you some money. I have some silver, take it, take it! *(Throwing coins on the table)* They're silver! No I didn't steal them. They were Judas's and he threw them in the thorns . . . I got scratched all over picking them up. Take them, you can take them since Judas hung himself over there. *(Pause)* Of course I want something from you in exchange. Let's make a deal. You give him *(Pointing to Christ)* to me, the permission to take him down and carry him away with me. Yes, Jesus Christ! For me! . . . No, not dead. You keep the dead. I want him still alive! Like he is now . . . he's breathing! *(Laughs happily)* Ha! Ha! You'll leave him for me? You're not worried! I know very well that if the centurions show up and discover an empty cross they'll clobber you one by one—a nail here, a nail there, one foot over the other. *(He makes gestures of hammering)* PAM! PAM!—I know, I know . . . but I'm proposing that we don't leave the cross empty, but put somebody else there in his place . . . Judas for example! Go get him down from the fig tree he's hanging from. Go get him . . . carry him here and stick him up there with four big nails. Nobody will notice the switch—everybody looks the same up on the cross, you know, they all turn into poor Christs. Is it a deal? Done! Go, go . . . No, I'll take care of Christ—I'll take Christ down by myself. Don't worry, I can do it, I'll use this ladder. *(Mimes taking the ladder and leaning it on the cross. [The giullare could also use an adjustable ladder that he leans against the arm of the cross.])* Jesus, pull in your little arm just a bit so I don't crush it. That's it, like that, now I'm coming . . . *(Climbing the rungs; happily)* Aha, aha . . . Jesus . . . You never thought that it would be a fool who would take you off the cross to save you. You save mankind and a fool saves you! Ha, ha, ha! What a joke we're pulling off! I'm coming . . . Don't worry. Now I'm going to take you down like a beautiful bride, sweet and precious . . . I'll carry you on my shoulders, then I'll take you on a boat that's there on the river, all the way to the far shore. When we get there, how sweet it will be . . .

there's a friend of mine over there who's a shaman. He has a lotion, a healing cream that when he spreads it all over you—GNAMM!—you'll be running around like a leper. Take it easy, Jesus! *(The wooden Christ moves in agitation)* Why are you trembling? Do you have a fever? Why are you shaking your head no? You don't want to? . . . You don't want to be un-nailed from here? Why? . . . Could you say that again, I didn't understand you! *(Pause)* . . . For the sacrifice? *(At a sustained rhythm)* Because you want to die on the cross . . . for the sacrifice, to save mankind from their sins, and in exchange for that you have to die nailed on the cross? Oh, oh, oh . . . And you say that I'm the fool? You're the fool, dammit! You and your whole family . . . starting with God the Father in person! And the big bird! The whole lot of you are fools! Ah, what a great idea, this Divine sacrifice! Do you know what priests are going to do to your holy martyrdom? They're going to picture it all in silver to mask your rotting flesh . . . they'll turn the drops of your blood into rubies . . . all set in gold . . . and the beams of wood of this cross will be bejeweled, perfumed and carried around so that all the poor people and peasants will throw themselves down onto their knees before it in mortification, flattened in devotion at the feet of the cross. And the priests that display it in procession will say: "Look at what he sacrificed for you! Get on your knees and make sacrifices too! On your knees, you sluggards!"

That is how the grand spectacle of your suffering will be used. Some salvation that is! Arms open like a bird, your image will be slapped onto shields and implements of war . . . and your cross will also be painted in vivid colors on banners. *(Again, at a sustained rhythm)* And it will be on the swords that slash and kill in the name of God and butcher women, men and all the children! There will be slaughter and massacres in the name of your sign! They'll use your sacrifice to perpetrate huge hoaxes and fraud . . . What? Say that again. You don't care how they exploit your passion . . . it would be enough if one man, clear-headed and blessed, took your teaching and used it for a holy cause? And who would be these worthy holy men? Give me some names! *(Pause)* Francis, good, Benedict, yes, Nicolas . . . all right! And after they have suffered every imaginable violence and indignity with the goal of comforting and rescuing from desperation the impoverished people who are downtrodden by the wealthy, how did they end up? Skewered alive and spit upon . . . then kicked around until they dropped dead. Jesus, what did you come on Earth to do? Did you come to teach us all that we would all be on a cross from the day we were born? Did you come to teach us all how to live nailed to a cross? No, that's not what we need. Excuse me, don't get angry, but we have no need for this lesson . . . You should teach us another lesson. Set an example that I've only seen you demonstrate to Christians one time. It was the day you went into the church and discovered the noble merchants buying, selling and haggling over merchandise, and you picked up a staff and—smack smack! Christ, that's what you should have taught us—to smack them! Smack them! Smack them! Smack them!

(The lights dim slowly as he exits beating a multitude of merchants.)

MARY UNDER THE CROSS

We come to the heart of *Mistero Buffo*—a classic, sacred mystery text.

I found the text of "Mary Under the Cross" before deciding to stage this show based on popular religion. I came across a magazine about medieval culture, which had published fragments of a text that had come to light during the renovation of the library at Montecassino. The writing was found on the back of a papyrus codex and consisted of a brief monologue by the Madonna, using terms that placed it in a dialect of southern central Italy. The scholars dated the text around the thirteenth century and noted that it was apparently a text taken from a sacred performance. This Madonna was very different from the traditional figure of the Virgin Mary: she in no way accepted the sacrifice that her son was making. On the contrary, she desperately opposed everyone who had participated in his being put on the cross. More than one commentator, analyzing this passion of the Virgin, has expressed the suspicion that it came from a performance by a group of heretics like the Cathars, reported by a monk as a form of provocation.

Later I showed the fragments in question to a friend who was a priest from Asti with a special interest in the tradition of popular religious theatre. My friend, the priest, procured for me another complete and analogous text, written in the Lombardi vernacular of the 1300s, but which could clearly be traced back to a performance whose origins were even older. Our priest informed me that in the twelfth century the tragic protest of the Madonna in this text resulted in a ferocious debate among the holy orders over this question: Was the Madonna aware that she would have to sacrifice her son for the sins of mortals or did she discover it in a brutal fashion only at the moment when she found her son on the cross?

There are several passages in the Gospels in which Jesus forewarns the apostles of his final sacrifice. He also repeats it to his minor followers. And in some Apocryphal Gospels he also tells Mary Magdalene, but no one records his having a conversation on this theme with his mother.

The tragic arc that we find in this piece, worthy of the Greek mystery plays, rises to an extraordinary level when the Madonna turns to the angel Gabriel to accuse him of having betrayed her by not warning her at the moment of the annunciation of the inhuman sacrifice that she would eventually have to endure.

Another highly theatrical passage is the one in which the Madonna climbs up on a ladder to persuade her son to come down from the cross. Along these lines there can be found a "contrasto" in an analogous laud from Cortona in which the Madonna insists that her son use his divine powers to liberate himself from this mortal tribulation. Mary tried every argument, but seeing that her son rejected all rational logic, she pushed Mary Magdalene under the cross and literally ripped off her clothes, leaving her chest bare. Then she shouted to her son: "Look at them! Behold those round firm breasts . . . you loved them when you had your feet on the ground! Come down. Don't lose this stupendous gift that she's offering to you."

There is definitely a provocation between the lines, at the limit of blasphemy, and it is not by chance that we also find it in other Umbrian lauds. This piece finds the greatest dramatic tension in the moment when the women following Jesus catch sight of the Holy Mother approaching Calvary in desperation. One of the women proposes that they throw a stone at her. Better that she be battered with blows than be devastated by grief for her son on the cross—a son who in his aching lamentations, in his gestures and in his supplications spoken in breathless exhaustion, does not appear to be an invulnerable God, but like the most normal of men, who suffers and trembles, not at all resigned to his death. It is here, in the same words used in the Gospel of Matthew, that Christ the man laments to his Father: "Lord, why have you forsaken me?"

The conclusion is given over to the dispute between the archangel and the Madonna who, as we have already noted, insults him by accusing him of having played a deceptive trick on her. And on the allegorical level we clearly sense that this insult is directed above all against the powers, both earthly and divine, which he represents. Both are authors of a ritual which sees as indispensable and unavoidable the sacrifice of her son.

It is obvious that the staging of this popular drama is not just about the killing of a human God. Throughout the entire mystery play, attention is given to the downtrodden, who always and continually suffer from oppression and tyranny. Humiliated and downtrodden, they use the voice of the Madonna to shout their revolt against supine acceptance, almost evoking the words of the Apocalypse that promise the coming of a better world, just and fair, where happiness can be enjoyed not only in the afterlife.

The mystery play of "Mary Under the Cross" will be performed by Franca in a dialect that combines various idioms from the Po valley. Perhaps some passages might escape you, but the musicality of the storytelling, as well as the gestures, will enable you to understand clearly the extraordinary atmosphere and provocation that the drama proposes to present to you.

———

First Woman enters running. She turns to other Women, who are standing under the cross.

FIRST WOMAN: Go and stop her . . . his mother is coming, the blessed Mary. Don't let her see him being crucified like a skinned goat, with fountains of blood streaming down all over him like springtime snow on a mountain . . . not to mention those huge nails that they hammered into the pained flesh of his hands and feet, piercing right through his bones!

THE WOMEN: Don't let her see him!

(Another Woman enters running.)

SECOND WOMAN: She won't stop . . . she's running so desperately that even the four sentinels can't stop her . . .

THIRD WOMAN: If they can't stop her with four, we have to try five . . . or six . . . she can't come here . . . she can't look at her son twisted like the roots of an olive tree devoured by ants.

FOURTH WOMAN: Hide him. At least cover up the face of the Son of God, so his mother can't recognize him . . . we can tell her it's the crucifix of someone else, a foreigner . . . that it's not her son!

FIRST WOMAN: I think that even if you cover him all over with a white sheet, his mother will recognize the Son of God all the same . . . all it will take is a toe popping out from under the sheet . . . a curl of his hair . . . because she made them. It's his mother.

(Another Woman enters out of breath.)

FIFTH WOMAN: She's coming . . . she's coming . . . the blessed Mary is here . . . it would be less painful to kill her with a knife than to let her see her son.

SIXTH WOMAN: Give me a rock to knock her over, so she'll fall to the ground and not risk seeing him!

(Mary enters. Her eyes go immediately to her son on the cross. Grief-stricken, she looks at him in wordless silence. The group of Women clear a path for her.)

FIRST WOMAN: Be quiet. Get over there . . . Oh, poor woman who is called blessed . . . how can she be blessed looking at that decoration impaled with four nails riveted into his pained flesh. You wouldn't even do that to a poisonous lizard or a bat.

SECOND WOMAN: Be quiet . . . hold your breath because now you will hear this woman scream at the top of her lungs, as if she had been ripped apart by grief . . . driven mad by the pain of seven blades piercing her heart!

THIRD WOMAN: She just stands there . . . she doesn't say anything. Let her cry a little at least. Let her scream, so she can burst through the heaviness that stifles her throat.

FOURTH WOMAN: Listen to the silence that causes great commotion—and there's no use covering your ears. *(Approaching Mary)* Speak, speak . . . say something,

Mary . . . cry, Mary . . . oh please . . . *(Almost shouting to shake her up, to end the terrible silence)* Speak, Mary!

MARY *(In a thin voice)*: Give me a ladder. I want to climb up close to my baby . . . *(She approaches the cross slowly, racked with pain, and speaks to her son)* Baby . . . oh, my beautiful pale son . . . Don't worry, my treasure, because now your mother is here . . . what have they done to you *(Gradually raising her voice)* Those murderers, pigs, butchers! *(Screams and runs around as if she sees the guilty ones)* What did he do to you, my big dimwit, to make you hate him so much, to make you treat him so wickedly! When I get my hands on you—one by one—I'll pay you back, even if I have to go looking for you to the ends of the Earth! Animals, beasts, wretches!

CHRIST *(Speaking through his exhaustion)*: Mamma . . . . Don't shout . . . Mamma.

MARY: Forgive me, my treasure, for being such a mess . . . and for shouting such wild words . . . but it's so unbearably painful to find you spattered with blood . . . all mangled . . . up on these poles . . . naked . . . battered with bruises . . . holes in those delicate little hands . . . and your feet . . . oh your feet! . . . dripping with blood, drop by drop! Oh, it must hurt so much!

CHRIST *(Between his words, his breath comes out in a rasping sound)*: No, Mamma . . . don't worry . . . now, I swear . . . I don't feel any more pain . . . I don't feel anything anymore . . . go home, Mamma, please . . . go home . . .

MARY: Yes, yes . . . let's go home together . . . I'll come up and get you down, take you down from these poles . . . *(Climbing up a ladder, which one of the bystanders has discreetly placed against the cross)* I'll pull out the nails one by one . . . *(Turns to the people standing around them)* Get me a pair of tongs . . . *(In desperation)* Can somebody help me!

(A Soldier enters.)

SOLDIER: Hey, woman, what are you doing up there on that ladder? Who gave you permission?

MARY: It's my son that you've nailed up there . . . I want to take him down and bring him home with me . . .

SOLDIER: Home? How considerate! He isn't ripe enough, holy woman . . . he's not yet fully seasoned! Dammit! Let's do it like this—as soon as he draws his last gasps, we'll whistle, and you can come get him all nicely wrapped-up, your dear boy. Happy? Now get down.

MARY: No I'm not coming down! I'm not going to let my son spend the night alone—and die! And you can't treat me so arrogantly . . . because I'm his mommy . . . I'm his mommy, I am!

SOLDIER: All right, dear Mommy, now you've busted my balls long enough! We're going to do what we do at apple picking time. You see? I'll give this ladder a good shake, and you'll come tumbling down like a ripe pear!

MARY *(A quick descent down the ladder)*: No, no . . . for pity's sake . . . wait until I get down. Look, I'm here at the bottom of the ladder.

SOLDIER: Oh, so in the end you understand how the game works, oh blessed woman! And don't look at me with those eyes crying fire, because I'm not the one to blame for putting this young man in that awkward position with his arms stretched out . . . You think I don't feel pity for you? You think I don't see those glistening bloodstained tears flowing down from your eyes? This is the grief of a mother! But I can't do anything. But there's nothing I can do because I have been ordered to carry out the punishment to the very end. I have been condemned to kill your child, or otherwise I will be nailed up there with the same nails.

MARY: Dear, kind, courteous Soldier, take this. I'll make you a gift of this gold ring and these silver earrings. Take them . . . in exchange for doing me a favor.

SOLDIER: What might that favor be?

MARY: To let me wash the blood off my son . . . with a little water and a rag . . . and also to moisten his lips cracked with thirst . . .

SOLDIER: Nothing more than those silly little things?

FIRST WOMAN: I'd also like to take this shawl and go up the ladder and put it around his shoulders, around his arms, to help him a little to bear the weight of the cross.

SOLDIER: Oh, woman, you must want to hurt your dear young boy, if you want to keep him alive longer to suffer that tremendous pain. If I were you, I'd do something to make Christ die faster.

MARY *(Realizing what the Soldier has said; almost whispering)*: Die? . . . Does he really have to die, my dear sweet thing? His hands die . . . his mouth die . . . his eyes . . . his hair die? *(In desperation, to herself)* Oh, how they have betrayed me. *(Calls out in a voice that gradually becomes more and more enraged. She turns her eyes to the sky)* Gabriel . . . Gabriel . . . Gabriel . . . young man with the kindly manner, first of all it was you, you! You betrayed me! With your sweet flowery voice you came to tell me that I would become a queen—me! Be blessed—me! Be joyous—me— above all other women! Look at me, look at me, falling to pieces and hoodwinked, the lowliest woman in the world! And you, you knew it when you first brought me the announcement, that melted me, that made my baby flower in my belly, that I would be brought to this beautiful throne of a queen! Queen! Queen, with a noble horseman for a son, with two spurs made out of big nails embedded in the flesh of his feet! Why didn't you give me a sign before? Oh, you can be sure I would have never wanted to become pregnant—no! Not under those conditions! Not even if God himself came in person, instead of sending that blessed spirit of the little white pigeon to marry me!

CHRIST: Mamma . . . oh, your pain drives you mad and makes you curse . . . *(To the Bystanders)* Bring her home, brothers . . . I beg you, bring her home before she falls over backwards . . .

BYSTANDER: Let's go, Mary, make your son happy, leave him in peace.

MARY: No, I don't want to! I'm sorry . . . let me stay here close to him . . . I won't say another bad word about his father . . . or anybody else. Let me stay . . . oh, be nice!

CHRIST *(Gasping with every breath he takes)*: I have to die . . .
Mamma . . . and it's difficult . . . I have to let myself go,
Mamma . . . consume the breath that keeps me alive . . .
but with you . . . down there . . . pulling your hair out . . .
I can't do it, Mamma . . . it makes it a lot harder for me.

MARY *(Imploring, almost voiceless)*: Don't chase me away,
Jesus! Don't chase me away! *(At the limit of desperation)*
I want to die, Jesus . . . I want to die . . . *(Shouts desperately to the Bystanders)* Suffocate me and bury me in a
tomb with my arms around my son! *(To Christ)* I want to
die, Jesus! I want to die . . .

SOLDIER: Holy woman, this mother's grief is too much to take.
Let's do it like this: we soldiers will pretend not to look.
You take this lance, thrust it with all your might through
his ribs into the bottom of his throat, then in a second,
you'll see, Christ will die.

(The Madonna faints and falls to the ground.)

What happened to you? She fainted and I didn't even
touch her?!

BYSTANDER: She had a fit, poor woman!

FIRST WOMAN: Stretch her out. Do it slowly and make space
around her so she can breathe.

SECOND WOMAN: Poor woman!

MARY *(As if in a dream)*: Who are you, young man, that you
look so familiar?

THIRD WOMAN: She's having visions!

GABRIEL: Gabriel, the angel of God. It's me, Virgin, the messenger from your lone and fragile love.

MARY *(In a thin voice, then gradually gaining force)*: Gabriel . . .
Gabriel . . . open your wings again, Gabriel . . . go back to
your beautiful and joyous heaven . . . there's nothing for
you to do here . . . on this filthy Earth . . . in this tortured
world. Go away, Gabriel . . . so you don't dirty your pastel-
colored wings . . . don't you see the mud and blood and
manure mixed with the stench of shit everywhere? . . . Go
away, Gabriel . . . so you don't befoul your delicate ears
with the desperate screams and tears and begging that

ring out everywhere . . . Go away, Gabriel . . . so you don't use up your luminous eyes looking at scabs and wounds . . . bubons and flies and worms oozing out of butchered corpses! You're not used to it, Gabriel . . . because there's no noise in heaven, no crying, no war, no prison, no lynched men, no raped women! No, there's no hunger, no famine, no one who sweats their guts out, no babies without smiles, no mothers blackened by grief . . . no one paying with pain for the sins of the world! Go away, Gabriel! Go away, Gabriel! *(Shouting)* Goooo awaaay, Gabrieeeel!

(The lights dim slowly to the sound of a Gregorian chant.)

THE STORY OF SAINT BENEDETTO OF NORCIA

PROLOGUE

Saint Benedetto of Norcia, as you know, is also known as the patron saint of masonry, which was his profession from the time he was a child. He is without a doubt the founder of organized monastic life. We are in the sixth century, which is to say the time of Totila the Goth and of Justinian, who was the leader of the Holy Roman Empire in the east.

The community of monks originally lived in old, abandoned houses, which they restored with the assistance of local peasants. To be a monk was to dedicate oneself to meditation, prayer, study and contemplation, but then Saint Benedetto changed things by requiring his followers to equip themselves with working tools so that they could labor in the fields, construct walls and build ovens for baking bread, pottery and bricks. This is the story of the transition from a life of prayer and contemplation to one of work and building in which the first rule of Benedetto's order was "pray and work."

But how did this change come to pass, this extraordinary adjustment?

It is a theme that has been recounted in many different keys, in the form of nursery rhymes, fables, giullare performances and morality plays from the high Middle Ages to the nineteenth century, often for satiric and didactic purposes. The version that we have reconstructed is surely among the oldest.

We have rewritten the giullare's story using the vernacular of southern central Italy as suggested by the few medieval fragments of popular memory from Umbria and Irpinia that were found.

—

GIULLARE: There was a time when the Benedictine monks lived in a cavern in the mountains. Oh, how majestic they were when they got down on their knees with their faces lifted to the heavens to pray and enjoy saintly visions! Their souls became so light that their bodies, liberated from the ordinary travails experienced by men and women, levitated into the air. And it sometimes happened that a holy man in prayer, lost in his celestial aura, could lift himself up off the ground and remain suspended there, for even half an hour.

All the monks began practicing ways to float in this miraculous state of suspension, and a tension grew among them as they competed with one another to see who could bob up the highest. These monks had discovered that a rigorous regimen of mystical training could empty their bodies of all burdens and enable them to levitate with ease. But if their thoughts returned to the normal troubles of everyday life they would immediately fall down to the floor with a big thud, a ruinous fall that left one severely bruised. Some of the monks who fluttered about, especially the youngest and most reckless ones, found themselves hanging in the air upside down. Then they would shake their feet and make somersaults in the sky.

"Bring me down to the ground!" they pleaded to their fellow monks. And those who had long poles hooked them as if they were birds, and brought them back down to earth. But one day it happened that the monk Serafino found himself fluttering lightly above the roof of the hermitage when he was hit by a gust of wind that carried him away like a sailboat tossed in a storm. He disappeared, floating away up into the highest clouds. The next week, four monks, in a state of desperation over the disappearance of their brother Serafino, were praying for the holy soul of the vanished one. And they were so lost in

Divine contemplation that they didn't notice they were rising up into the sky, and were almost knocked senseless by a flock of migrating swallows.

"Come down here! Come down!" shouted the monks below, but they were drunk with beatitude and deaf as bats. The little monks kept straying farther up into the sky, until they slowly disappeared into the firmament. All the monks were now crying inconsolably, and the holy father Benedetto issued an order that every monk, when praying, would be required to keep a heavy stone in his pocket.

But that wasn't enough, because the monks would still take flight every day, as if they were buzzards or finches. So these holy men tried to wrap a rope around their bellies that tied them to an anchor of dead weight. Others tied the rope to a tree. But it was no use: the moorings were uprooted by the winds, and the monks continued soaring away into the clouds!

The monk who worked in the kitchen, who was called Cook, tied a rope around his neck that he attached to a wagon. He rose up in flight, but could not free himself from the rope, which was tied to the wagon and held him back. He was saved, but his fellow monks found him strangled, hanging from his neck.

At this point the holy leader, Benedetto, called all the monks to a meeting and said: "We have to come up with a solution . . . you all know that if even our brother Cookie, who prepares our food, flies away into the sky, we are in big trouble. Before long no one will be left! It is clear that we are having no success in trying to save ourselves with stones, anchors, or by tying ourselves to wagons. The only true anchor that can save us is this!" And the holy man took a shovel that was leaning against the wall, put it in the hands of a monk, and said: "Here! Hold this tool and you won't levitate into the sky anymore."

"Holy Master," said the monk Boniface, "this shovel is not heavy enough to serve as mooring!"

"That's true, if you let it hang there in your hands! But if you try to dig it into the ground, and push into it with

your feet, and lift up clumps of earth, over and over
again, you will quickly discover how heavy it is, and how
it weighs you down! Let's all try to take up a hoe or a rake,
and you others, try a pole or a pitchfork. Put your arms
and your back into it. Dig into the earth and crush the
stones. Push the wagons, build walls, construct arches to
buttress them. Build a round wall around that cellar to
make an oven for bread and bricks. Be strong! . . . Get
moving! Push harder! . . . Crush it! . . . Lift! . . . Scrape! . . .
Keep going! Now listen to the sweat that falls drop by
drop from your forehead to your arms, and that way you
can be sure that you won't be able to levitate even an inch
into the air!

"From now on, my monks, it is up to us to earn our
bread and the right to live in this world.

"You want a roof? Walls around your cells to keep you
fresh and protected? Build them! You want grains and
fruits? Hoe the ground and plant them!

"We no longer have the right to weigh down the shoulders of others, peasants and poor people, with the clever
blackmail that we pray and sing glory to their souls while
they labor to fill our bellies! Give up that game . . . and we
will remain blessed with our feet planted firmly on the
ground! Amen!"

DEATH AND THE FOOL

PROLOGUE

Now we come to the piece performed by the giullari that is called "Death and the Fool." This text is of Croatian origin, but we have found it in a Dalmatian transcription that is fairly old. "Fool," "fou," "balengo," "luch," "loco," etc., are some of the terms and expressions found in numerous European countries that refer to a masked character: the one representing folly, in fact.

In the popular theatre of past ages the fool is a character of contradiction, counterpoint and reversal. He operated beyond the rules and accepted neither custom nor logic . . . not to mention anything else dictated by social standards, laws or absolute dogma. In short, he is the allegoric representation of disorder and transgression.

There is also a famous text by Erasmus of Rotterdam that discusses "The Ship of Fools." The satiric text was inspired by an actual medieval custom. In the beginning of spring in the Anseatic Republic, all the madmen, deviants, giullari and oddballs, including heretics, liberal thinkers and unregulated prostitutes, were forced to embark on a ship that had been stripped of its rudder and set adrift. The vessel was towed into the open sea and left to the prevailing currents that inevitably took it to the north into the ice of the Baltic Sea. It was a convenient way of eliminating all the ballbreakers, the ones who stood out from the crowd.

We find the fool in many sacred stories: he is the character we meet at the tavern in Emmaus, precisely on the night of the famous supper, the last one. Jesus Christ and his apostles are in a room of their own, while the fool and the regular customers are in a room next to the kitchen. Playing cards around a big table are a priest, a soldier, a merchant. It is clear that they are meant to be allegorical characters that suggest professions of power. Also with them is a fool who is naturally destined to lose every hand. The fool, who represents the common people, insists on playing with the hope that he will win at least a few hands, but the rules are made by the three others in charge of the game, who cheat brazenly and hide cards in every fold of their clothing—it's impossible to beat them!

From the other room (offstage) one can occasionally hear noises: a stifled laugh, overlapping voices, a confused dialogue of saints who get themselves worked up in heated discussions. A brief altercation breaks out involving Judas, who takes offense and walks out slamming the door. Some of the followers run out after him, trying to calm him down and convince him to go back into the banquet room: "Come on, don't be like that. He didn't mean it . . . you know how he is, every so often he gets bent out of shape and comes down hard on someone, but he doesn't do it out of mean-ness. He probably wasn't thinking, or if you ask me—he was only joking! Come back in, come on . . . you'll see, he'll probably even apologize!" And Judas goes back in, supported by four apostles.

We note the servants passing by with basins full of water: "Strange people," observes the fool glancing into the other room. "How original! They wash their feet before eating." The door keeps opening and closing . . . the fool keeps looking in through the door-way, and every once in a while makes gestures of greeting to Jesus. He winks his eye and says, "What a nice guy Christ is!"

At a certain point the hall is shaken by a blast of frigid air that makes the curtains quiver . . . a strange figure enters the scene . . . a woman covered by an enormous black cloak, bordered with ragged tassels, with a veil on her head that makes it hard to see her face. She carries a scythe—it is "the Grim Reaper": Death. Chilled by goosebumps, the players around the table ran away, running or crawling along the wall. The hostess and the servants withdraw, locking themselves in the kitchen. The only one left in the room is the fool. He is shocked, staring at the Grim Reaper, who approaches him and sits down across from him. The fool, although a little late, recognizes her. He is convinced that she has come for him, but he tries to appear nonchalant, even playing the braggart: "You shouldn't have gone to all this trouble to take away a good-for-nothing like me ... I could understand if you were hunting for a big shot, some filthy-rich moneybags!"

Almost immediately the fool realized that Death was not interested in him, but that the dark lady had come to take Jesus Christ. The two spoke for a while and the veiled woman made it clear what would become of Jesus. He couldn't breathe or hold back his tears, and then all of a sudden, with the unpredictability of an authentic madman, he burst out into laughter and began to sing, leaping up and down all over the room ... offering a drink to the Grim Reaper, exasperatedly courting her with paradoxical compliments. The said veiled woman was incredulous, but entertained, toasting and drinking with the fool. But as it is known: Death doesn't know how to hold its wine. After a while we see her laughing and dancing, almost vulgarly, held around the waist by the fool, who twirls her like a puppet. Amidst the swirling veils, tassels and cloaks, appeared the pallid face of the queen of the graveyard: "Oh, my pale beauty," exclaimed the fool. Her firm white breasts were exposed. The fool caressed her and dizzied her with words, squeezed her close to him, lifted her up and made her fly. The pale beauty was weakened with languor. She was losing her head over this madman, and left embracing him, chirping like a magpie in love.

The allegory is ancient, dating back without doubt to pre-Christian times. It obviously alludes to a ritual that sees the fool as Christ's double, who conquers Death, including suffering a burial, since he, immortal, sacrifices himself and dies to free mankind.

Now we will present a fragment of this scene performed entirely in dialogue. The piece would normally be staged by at least six actors.

—

At an inn some idlers play cards with the Fool.

FOOL: The horse on the ass, the virgin over the sinner, and I take it all home! Ah, ah. You always thought I was a chicken waiting to be plucked, eh? And now, how do things stack up? *(Deals the cards)*

FIRST PLAYER: The game's not over . . . wait a minute before you start singing.

FOOL: No, I'll sing no matter what . . . and dance! *(Looking at his cards)* Oh what beautiful cards! Good evening, Your Majesty, Mister King . . . would you mind helping me take the crown from this big bastard friend of mine? *(Slaps a card onto the table)*

SECOND PLAYER: Ah, ah . . . you fell into a trap with the king. Now I'm going to put down the emperor!

FOOL: Ohi, ohi—you look at what I'm going to do to this emperor: I'm going to beat him with this *(Turns his back and puts his buttocks on the table)* and then I'll add this killer who will butcher the emperor like a hog.

FIRST PLAYER: And I'll stop the killer with the captain . . .

FOOL: And I'll start a war, so the captain will have to leave!

SECOND PLAYER: And I'll bring on famine, cholera and plague to end the war!

FOOL: And then you'll have to get an umbrella because I'm spitting out tempests and storms . . . I'm spitting out rain and floods! *(Drinks from a goblet and sprays everyone)*

FIRST PLAYER: Oh you miserable foolhardy wretch, what kind of fool are you?

FOOL: I'm the kind of fool they call foolhardy . . . I'm utterly foolish . . . and I win this round of tarot cards with the flood that sends all pestilence packing.

HOSTESS: Stop making all this racket. I have people sitting down to eat in the banquet hall.

FOOL: Who are they?

HOSTESS: I don't know . . . I never saw them in Emmaus at my inn. They call them apostles.

(They stop their game for a moment.)

SECOND PLAYER: Ah, they're the twelve that follow around that man from Nazareth.

FOOL: Yes, Jesus, who would be the one in the middle; look over there . . . he seems like a nice guy to me! *(Calls out in a loud voice)* Oh, Jesus of Nazareth, I salute you! Bon appétit! *(To his friends)* Did you see? He winked at me . . . what a nice guy!

THIRD PLAYER: Twelve and one makes thirteen . . . thirteen at a table is bad luck!

FOOL: Oh, they're crazy! Wait while I cast a counter-spell to chase away the evil eye.

(Sings:)

> Dinner for thirteen's
> Not as bad luck as it might seem
> So, evil eye, get outta here fast
> Before I kick you in your ass.

(He pinches the Hostess's ass.)

HOSTESS: Be good, foolhardy Fool, or you'll make me spill this boiling water!

FIRST PLAYER: Boiling water? What are they going to do with that? *(Deals the cards)*

HOSTESS: I think they're going to wash their feet.

SECOND PLAYER: Wash their feet before they eat? Oh, they're definitely out of their minds! Foolhardy Fool, you better go over there with them, because they're the kind of companions that were made just for you.

(In the confusion of the conversation, the Fool doesn't realize that his companions are quickly switching the cards.)

FOOL: You said it . . . you're right. I'll win this hand and with the loot you pay me I'll go over to the banquet hall and drink with them . . . and you won't come since you're not fools or foolhardy . . . you are very wise sons of thieves and whores!

THIRD PLAYER: Play, play . . . I really want to enjoy your victory!

FOOL: Speaking of thieves, what happened to the card of the fool that I had in my hand?

SECOND PLAYER: Give him a mirror so he can look into it; you'll find the face of the fool there right away.

FIRST PLAYER: Stop stalling and play! *(Starts the game)* The horseman with his sword!

SECOND PLAYER: The queen with her staff!

FOOL: The witch with her gourd!

THIRD PLAYER: The baby who's innocent!

FIRST PLAYER: God who's omnipotent.

FOOL: Justice and reason!

SECOND PLAYER: The lawyer who's a smart fellow!

THIRD PLAYER: The hanged man on the gallows!

FOOL: The pope and the popess!

FIRST PLAYER: The priest who says mass!

SECOND PLAYER: Life, gay and joyful!

THIRD PLAYER: Death, black and tearful!

SECOND PLAYER:

>That's the last card, how very shrewd.
>My dear, Mr. Fool, it looks like you're screwed.

FOOL: How is it possible! How did I manage to lose?

FIRST PLAYER: How did you manage? You can't play, dear Mr. foolhardy prick of a fool. Now pay up. Out with the money.

FOOL: You've completely wiped me out . . . but I could have sworn that I had it myself, that card of death . . . I remember it was right here in the middle.

(Death appears against the backdrop wrapped in a large black cloak. A light veil partially reveals a deathly pale face.)

SECOND PLAYER: Oh, mamma . . . who's that?

(The Fool turns his back on Death. He is intent on counting what little money he has left.)

THIRD PLAYER: The Grim Reaper . . . Death!

(Everyone runs away except the Fool.)

FOOL: Yes, Death! Exactly . . . I had it myself! Oh, it's cold in here . . . Where did you all hide? I have a chill that's freezing me down to my bones. Close that door . . . *(Barely catches sight of Death)* Good day! *(To himself)* It's all closed up . . . where is this damned draft coming from? *(Fixes his attention on the veiled woman and has a sudden fright)* Good day, good evening . . . good night . . . excuse me, madam. *(Stands up to leave but does not know how to say good-bye)* Since my friends have gone . . . *(Realizes that he forgot his money on the table, so he stops himself and turns back)* Are you looking for someone? The proprietress is there in the banquet room serving the apostles at the table, and the basins for washing their feet . . . if you want to go, don't stand on ceremony. *(Trembles visibly)* Oh, what chattering teeth!

DEATH: No, thank you, but I prefer to wait here.

FOOL: Fine . . . if you want to sit down, take this chair . . . it's still warm, I warmed it up myself! *(The woman sits)* Excuse me, ma'am, but now that I see you up close it seems that I've met you some other time.

DEATH: That's impossible, because I'm someone that one meets only once.

FOOL: Oh, yes? Only once? You have an out-of-towner's accent . . . it sounds to me like Tuscan. *(The woman shakes her head no)* It's not? Ferrarese? Roman? Trevigian? Sicilian? How about Cremonian? In any case, ma'am, may I say that you seem a little under the weather, a little pallid . . . since the last time I didn't meet you.

DEATH: You think I'm pallid?

FOOL: Yes, I hope that doesn't offend you?

DEATH: No, I've been eternally pallid? Pallor is my natural color.

FOOL: Naturally pallid? *(Suddenly he remembers)* Ah, that's who you look like! *(He takes a card from the deck and shows her)* You're the spitting image of the figure painted on this card.

DEATH: Exactly. I am Death.

FOOL: Death? *(Stammering)* Ah, you are Death, you? *(His legs shake visibly)* Look what a coincidence! It's Death! Very good . . . a pleasure to meet you . . . I'm the foolhardy fool.

DEATH: Do I frighten you?

FOOL: Frighten me? *(Does not succeed in controlling the continuous trembling of his legs)* No, I'm a fool and everybody knows, even in the tarot cards, that the fool has no fear of

149

Death. In fact, to the contrary, he goes looking for her to match up as a couple, because together they beat all the other cards, even Love!

DEATH: If you're not afraid, why is your leg trembling?

FOOL: My leg? It's because this leg is not mine. I lost my real leg on a battlefield . . . so I borrowed one from a captain . . . who was dead and his leg was still moving around like the tail of a freshly killed lizard. And so I cut off his leg and stuck it on myself, with spit . . . *(He moves, miming the gait of a cripple)* so look, it's clear to see this can't be mine . . . it's quite a bit longer than the other one, and makes me limp. *(He turns to the leg which continues to tremble)* Oh! Stay put, you shouldn't be afraid of an illustrious lady Madonna like this! *(As if speaking to a horse)* Come on now, take it easy!

DEATH: You are very kind to call me an illustrious Madonna.

FOOL: Oh, no I'm not doing it to be polite, believe me . . . it's just that to me, I swear, you are illustrious and even adorable. I'm flattered that you have come to visit me . . . and I like you, so much so, that I'd be happy to buy you a drink, if you'd let me!

DEATH: With pleasure . . . *(Interested)* Did you say you liked me?

FOOL *(Pouring wine into glasses)*: Of course! I like everything about you: the aroma of chrysanthemums that hovers around you . . . the colorless pallor of your face . . . you know what they say:

A woman whose skin is as white as a dove,
Is a woman who never gets tired of making love.

DEATH: Oh, you're embarrassing me. You're a fool that lives up to his name. No one ever made me blush like this before.

FOOL: You blush because you are a chaste and pure woman; it's true that you have embraced many men, but each only once . . . because none of them deserved to be held and caressed in your arms . . . because none of them treated you with true love and esteem.

150   DEATH: It's true, no one esteems me!

FOOL: Because you are too modest and don't sound the trumpets or beat the drums to announce you're coming, though you deserve all that as a queen . . . *(Pours a drink)* Queen of the world! *(Raises a glass in a toast)* To your health, Queen!

DEATH: To the health of Death? I don't know if you are more of a fool or a poet.

FOOL: Both, because every true poet is a fool, and vice versa. *(Offers her a drink)* Drink, pale lady, this wine will give you a little color.

(They drink.)

DEATH *(Sipping her drink)*: Oh, how delicious!

FOOL: And how could it not be delicious? It's the same thing that the man from Nazareth is drinking over there in the banquet hall . . . and that one knows his wine . . . he's a regular connoisseur!

DEATH: Which of them is the one from Nazareth?

FOOL: The young one sitting in the middle, the one with the big clear eyes.

DEATH: He's a man of fine bearing!

FOOL: Yes, he's a good-looking young man, but you don't want to make me jealous? You don't want to insult me by leaving me alone to go with them . . . that would make me cry in desperation!

DEATH: Are you trying to flatter me, you clever man?

(She removes her veil, revealing long golden hair, an extremely pallid face, and sweetly shaded eyes. She is very beautiful.)

FOOL: Me flatter you? Flatter a lady who holds sway over popes and emperors? Oh! Your hair is so enchanting that I would happily gather all the flowers of the earth and throw them onto you until you were all covered up in a huge bouquet, and then I'd throw myself into that bouquet to look for you so I could take off all the flowers, and everything else too!

DEATH: You are making me grow very hot with these words, my dear Fool . . . and I'm sorry . . . because I would have been happy to have remained in your company and to have taken you with me.

FOOL: That's not what you came for . . . to carry me away? *(Laughs happily)* Ah! You didn't come for me . . . Ha, ha . . . And I thought . . . Oh, that's good for a big laugh, that is! What a riot! That switch is fine with me! I'm very happy! Ha, ha!

DEATH: Now I see your game clearly, liar . . . you feigned amorous passion to soften me up and slip away from Death . . . which is who I am.

FOOL: No, you've got it all wrong, white lady . . . I'm celebrating the fact that you are not here with me on official business . . . you haven't chosen my company just to practice your profession of drawing out the last breath . . . but because I won your eyes and your heart through the pleasure that I give you . . . isn't that true? You think I'm nice, don't you, Snow White? Tell me? *(Brief pause)* What's happening to you . . . all those big teardrops coming down from your eyes? This is the height of folly! Death crying! Did I offend you?

DEATH: No, you did not offend me . . . you . . . melted my heart with tenderness. I'm crying with melancholy for that boy Jesus who is so sweet . . . because he is the one whose breath I must take away.

FOOL: Oh, it's him you've come for . . . for Christ! Dammit, I'm sorry too, poor kid. And through what accident or sickness will you take him away with you?

DEATH: The sickness of the cross . . .

FOOL: Of the cross? He's going to end up nailed to it? Oh, poor Christ . . . he couldn't have a more unlucky name! Listen, pale face, do me a favor, let me go and warn him . . . so he can prepare himself for this awful torture.

DEATH: It's useless to warn him, because he knows already . . . he's known since birth that tomorrow he will be stretched out on the cross.

FOOL: He knows . . . he knows it and still sits there calmly, smiling blessedly at his companions? Oh, he's a bigger fool than I am.

DEATH: You said it! Come . . . let's not think about it anymore . . . come pour me some wine, because I want to get drunk . . . and get far away from this sadness.

FOOL: You're right . . . it's better to have a happy Death! So let's drink and chase away the blues! Lovely white lady . . . come and let's make ourselves crazy with joy . . . unhook your cloak so I can savor those firm arms the color of the moon . . . *(She takes off her cloak)* Oh, how precious they are! Unhook the front of your jacket too, so I can feast me eyes on those two silver apples that look like the stars of Diana . . .

DEATH: No, please, Fool . . . I'm young and inexperienced and I'm feeling ashamed . . . because no man has ever touched me nude!

FOOL: But I'm the fool, not a man . . . and Death commits no sin if she's loved by a silly fool like me. Don't worry, because I'll put out all the lights but one . . . and we'll dance . . . the beautiful steps that I want to teach you that will make you sing sighs and moans of love. *(Sings to the beat of the dance steps that spin faster and faster:)*

> Let yourself go, and keep spinning around
> So my fingers can dance in the folds of your gown
> Let me dance my way inside of your thighs
> And let both your legs wrap themselves around mine
> Let's both take a ride on a merry-go-round
> We'll let our heads spin, and turn the world upside down!

BONIFACE VIII

And now we come to Boniface VIII, the pope during the time of Dante. Dante knew him well: he hated him so much that he sent him to the inferno even before he was dead. Another one who hated him, but in a slightly different manner, was the Franciscan monk Jacopone da Todi, an evangelical advocate of pauperism, whom we would call today an extremist. He was linked to all the movements of poor peasants, especially in his region, so much so that in contempt of the laws of prevarication imposed by Boniface VIII, who was a real thief, he shouted in one of his cantos: "Ha! Boniface, you have turned the Church into a whore!" Boniface didn't forget . . . when he finally succeeded in getting his hands on Jacopone, who was among other things an extraordinary man of the theatre, he threw him into jail, sitting, forced to remain in this position— *(Demonstrates)* hands together and feet tied, for five years, chained on top of his own feces. And it is said that after five years, when he was freed, thanks to the sudden death of the pope, this poor monk, still very young, was no longer able to walk. He was forced to drag himself around folded in two. When, a year and a half later, he died, and they tried to stretch him out in his coffin, they couldn't do it; every time they stretched him out—Gniiii!—he snapped back into the original position. In the end they got tired of trying and just buried him sitting down.

And he was not the only one who hated the pope. There was also Gioacchino da Fiore, who lived before Saint Francis and was considered as a kind of father to all heretical movements. He more or less said: "If we want to give dignity to the Church of Christ, we have to destroy the Church—the huge beast of Rome, the awful beast of Rome. And to destroy the Church it is not enough to knock down the walls, the roofs, the bell towers; we also have to destroy those who govern it: the pope, the bishops, the cardinals." His position was a little radical. In fact, the pope of his time immediately sent a welcoming party of hundreds of soldiers to go looking for him in the mountains where he lived. Thanks to a spy, they located the cave where he resided, but, unfortunately for them, they found him dead—still warm, but dead. He had died two minutes before their arrival. No one knows if it was out of fear from seeing the soldiers coming, or if he was just being nasty and wanted to display his contempt for them. I think that was it: Gioacchino da Fiore was spiteful, very spiteful.

Look at this image of Boniface VIII. *(Shows painting)* It is very realistic: we see him using the monk, Segalello da Parma, as a seat. Segalello da Parma was in the order of the "sackers" (who were given this name because they dressed themselves in sacks). He was another extremist.

The extremist, who was used as a seat, was one of those demanding that the pope and the Church be poor, extremely poor, that everything be put into the hands of people who were more humble because: "The dignity of the Church," said Segalello, "should be based on the dignity of the poor." When you, Church, have among your members a poor wretch who dies of hunger, you are a Church that should not glorify yourself with continued life!

As for his nickname, the people called him Segarello.[3] Segalello was one of those who preached absolute chastity, and his nickname evidently came from the fact that he was never seen going around with women. In any case, this monk with a nickname that could almost be that of a "giullare," went around provoking the peasants: "Hey, you, what are you doing? Playing? Oh no! Shoveling the land? You're working! And who does the land belong to? I imagine it's yours! No? It's not yours? But why not? You work the land and ... But you make a profit from it? What profit? Ha, that small a percentage? And what's that, all the rest is kept by the master? The

3. In Italian, "Segarello" is slang for someone who masturbates.

master of what! Of the land? Ha ha ha! There is a master of the land? Do you really believe that in the Bible such and such a plot of land is allocated to mister such and such ... you fools! Ignoramuses! The land is yours: they took it away, and then they made you do all the work. The land belongs to those who work it! Is that clear?"

Think of it, in the Middle Ages, to go around saying things like that: "The land belongs to those who work it!" You have to be out of your mind to say it today—let alone in the Middle Ages! In fact, they immediately put him on the torture rack, him and his entire band of "sackers."

Only one escaped. He was called Brother Dolcino, and he retreated to his homeland, in the area of Vercelli, but instead of staying at his house in silence, and in spite of the risk it entailed, he went around provoking the peasants by performing as a giullare. He would begin: "Hey, peasants! ... The land is yours. Take it, you imbecilic fools, the land belongs to those who work it ..."

And the peasants from Vercelli, maybe because he spoke their dialect and they understood him well, looked at him and said: "Hey, hey ... Brother Dolcino is out of his mind! But the things he says are not so crazy! You know I think I'll keep the land for myself ... No, on the contrary, I'll leave the land to the master, but I'll keep the crops!" And from that day on, every time the collectors arrived, they threw stones at them. And they even began to rip up their contracts that were called "tyrannies." Yes, the contracts that linked the peasants to the masters in the Middle Ages were called "tyrannies." Once that word had only one meaning: a contract. But then people began to understand, and it was enriched with other shades of significance: "Ah, a tyranny? . . ." that is, a contract between a peasant and a master. So they tore up the contract. But knowing that they couldn't resist on their own, they united, they formed associations with one another, all the peasants in the area. Not only that, but they understood that they had to enlarge their union in order to increase their power, so they banded together with poor artisans and wage earners, who, in the Middle Ages, were beginning to exist in large numbers. And in this way they formed an extraordinary community organization. Among themselves they called each other "communitarians."

They are the first communitarians in history that we know of. As a center of organization they had what they called a "credenza."

Today credenzas exist all over Italy, from Sicily to Veneto. It is the cupboard that we keep in the house to store things to eat. The noun evidently comes from the verb "credere": to believe, to believe in something, to have credence in something. Therefore "credenza" is to have credence in and believe in a community. These forms of communities came into existence in the sixth century. The first credenza of which we have news is the credenza in the community of Saint Ambrogio: an enormous cupboard, immense, made in the style of a ship's hold, with lots of little doors made of a special wood that preserved grain from humidity and kept the rest of the community's food well-preserved, as with everything that would be needed by the community in times of famine.

So there in Vercelli, because of the common sharing of goods, there was no possibility of famine: they gathered together everything that there was and distributed it to everyone according to their needs. Note that well. According to need, not according to the work that each of them had produced.

This type of self-governing was very annoying to the masters, above all to those who felt that they had been robbed of their land. One in particular, the Count of Monferrato, organized a punitive expedition. Left with his henchmen, he caught a hundred of the communitarians and cut off their hands and feet. It was a throwback to earlier times, when in Britain, two hundred years earlier, the lords had done the same thing to their peasants. Hands and feet cut off, they were put on the backs of donkeys and driven towards the city of Vercelli, so the communitarians could see what would happen to those who were presumptuous enough to take too many liberties.

When the communitarians saw their own brothers battered and deformed in this way they did not sit down and cry. They left that same night and took Novara by surprise, entering the city and making a true and proper massacre of the henchmen, the murderous executioners. Not only that, they also succeeded in convincing the population to free themselves and to organize a community of their own. With incredible speed there were rebellions in Oleggio, Pombia, Castelletto Ticino, Arona, all the northern part of Lago Maggiore, Domodossola, the area near Monte Rosa, all of Lago d'Orta, la Valsesia, Varallo, la Val Mastallone, Ivrea, Biella, Alessandria ... in short, half of Lombardi and Piemonte. Throwing their hands up in dismay, the dukes and counts sent a messenger to Rome, who arrived shouting to the pope: "Help, help . . . you've got to help us, for God's sake!" Faced with doing something "for God's sake" what choice did the pope have? "For pity's sake, for God's sake, I have to help them . . ." Fortunately for him and for the lords of the north, preparations were being made in Brindisi to embark on the Fourth Crusade (the one we know nothing about, because it was conducted in total secrecy, and about which we are told things which really took place in the fifth one). And so he sent a message to the crusaders: "Stop everything. Excuse me. I made a mistake. The infidels are not on the other side of the sea. They're up there in Lombardi, dressed up as peasant rebels. Go there right away!" By forced march, eight thousand men (almost all of them German) arrived in Lombardi where they joined with the troops of the dukes of Visconti, Modrone, Torriani, Borromeo, and with those of the Count of Monferrato (there were also two new characters, the Savoys, who were just then coming into their own), and they launched a ferocious massacre. They succeeded in ambushing three thousand communitarians on a mountain near Biella—men, women and children. In a single blow they massacred them all; they set them aflame, they butchered them . . .

These stories, which I have briefly summarized for you, are not recorded in the books used in schools. And it makes sense on one hand: Who organizes culture? Who decides what to teach? In whose interest is it to withhold certain information? The wealthy, the bourgeoisie. As long as they are allowed to do so, it is natural that they will do what they believe is in their interests. Can you imagine that these people will lose their heads and begin telling everyone all about an actual revolution that took place in trecento Lombardi and Piemonte, during which, in the name of Christ, a community was built where everyone was equal, loved each other and didn't exploit anyone? There's the possibility that children might rejoice and shout: "Long live Brother Dolcino! Down with the pope!" No, that can't be allowed. For God's sake, that can't be allowed!

I'm exaggerating of course, for the love of polemics, because, to tell the truth, in some of the more advanced textbooks, in some schools with grand traditions (the Berchet, for example, which my son attends), mention of these events can be found. There was even a footnote that said (I'm citing from memory): "In 1306,

Brother Dolcino, a heretic, was burned alive with his mistress." Do you understand? In this way children learn that Brother Dolcino was a heretic and that he also had a mistress!

Now I am going to perform the piece about Boniface VIII. It begins with a very old extra-liturgical Catalan chant, from the area of the Pirenei. During the chant, the pope dresses himself for an important ceremony. The piece refers to a vice that Boniface was known for. In certain cities he would nail monks by their tongues to the main doors of the noblemen's houses. That is because these monks advocating pauperism or linked to other heretical movements like the Cathars, had the bad habit of going around speaking ill of the aristocrats. So the pope took them and—ZACK— *(Mimes the act of hammering a nail through a tongue)* Not him personally. He was actually afraid of blood. But he had men assigned especially to the job. He knew how to delegate!

Another episode that is remembered about him, just to give you an idea of what type of man he was, is the orgy that was held on Good Friday in 1301. Among the many processions that were held in Rome that day, there was one by the Cathars, who took advantage of the liturgical chanting to insult the pope with lines sung under their breath. They said: "Jesus Christ was a poor man who walked around without even a cloak. There is on the other hand someone who has a cloak, and it is full of precious jewels. There is someone who sits on a throne of gold, while Christ walked on bare feet. Christ, who was God, the Heavenly Father, descended to the earth to be a man, while there is someone who is not even a man, who likens himself to the Heavenly Father, and to be God has himself carried around on a palanquin . . ."

For pity's sake! Boniface, who knew what was going on, thought, "You want to bet that they are angry with me? Do you? I will prepare something to offend everyone!" He organized an orgy right on Good Friday: he invited some prostitutes, some ladies from good families (which often is the same thing), bishops and cardinals, and it seems that all of them did things that were sordid and undignified—so much so that all the courts of Europe were scandalized, even that of Henry III of England, who, according to the historians of the time, was a rather crude king.

In fact, they say that to entertain his barons during banquets he would put out a candle with a burp from three-meters' distance!

Someone even added—but I don't believe it—that he was even able to put them out on a rebound with a ricochet, which is to say that he would burp towards a wall ... and then like in billiards ... *(He mimes a billiards shot)* TACK-TICK. This, of course, is British humor, and we aren't capable of appreciating all the subtleties; it's like cricket.

The Giullare, through his actions, gives the impression that he is surrounded by choirboys, singers who dress him up for the procession which is about to take place shortly. He mimes the gestures of praying. He sings:

GIULLARE:
>Al Jorn del Judici
>Parra Qui Avra Fet Servici
>Un Rey Vindra Perpetual
>Vestit de Nostra Carn Mortal
>Del Ziel Vindra Toti Sertament
>Al Jorn ...

>*(On the day of judgment*
>*There will appear one who will serve us*
>*An eternal king will come*
>*Dressed in our mortal flesh*
>*From the sky he will surely come*
>*On the day ...)*

(He interrupts himself and turns to one of his imaginary choirboys) The hat ... *(He goes back to singing:)*

>Al Jorn ...

(He interrupts himself and turns to an imaginary choirboy) The big hat, the big one ... *(Goes back to singing:)*

>Del Judici
>Un Gran Senial Sa Monstrara ...

(On the day of judgment
A great sign will be made manifest . . .)

(He takes the miter from the hands of the choirboys and·
puts it on his head. He immediately takes it off.)

Ahia! Damn you, little wretch, it's made of iron! Are you trying to smash my head! Do you think I'm getting dressed to fight a war? *(He always interweaves his orders into the Gregorian chant)* Give me the light one because I'm just going for a walk . . . *(He takes another head covering)* This one will be fine . . . *(He puts it on his head and continues singing:)*

Al Jorn del Judici . . .

(He interrupts himself, giving an order) The mirror . . .
(Looking at himself in the mirror with satisfaction) Glove! *(Goes back to singing:)*

Al Jorn del Judici . . .

(Ordering) Glove!!! *(Annoyed)* The other one . . . Only one glove!! I have another hand . . . Do you want me to cut it off? *(Mimes having one arm with a stump)*

(He goes back to the song as he puts on the glove, and using the notes of the song, he counts the number of his fingers, which the first time through results in his having too many. He repeats the counting, still using the scales of the song, and is reassured to discover that he does actually have five fingers on each hand. Satisfied, he executes a festive crescendo. Giving orders:)

The cloak! . . . The big cloak . . . The big one, the one covered with jewels set in silver and gold. *(Sings:)*

Al Jorn del Judici
Parra Qui Avra . . .

Bring it here! There's five of you choirboys, dammit! . . .
Lift up the cloak. You're getting it all dirty dragging it on
the ground; let's go! Eh, did you drink too much curdled
milk today! *(Takes a large heavy cloak from the choirboys)*
Oh, this is a heavy one! *(Returns to singing, as he tries
unsuccessfully to place the cloak on his shoulders)*

Parra Qui Avra Fet Servici . . .

(Giving orders) Help me get this onto my shoulders! *(Sings:)*

Parra Qui Avra Fet Servici . . .

Come on, get it up there! Give it a shove *(The force of the
shove makes him sing off-key. He stops and turns to the
choirboys lowering the cloak)* Dammit! Do I have to do
everything myself? . . . Am I a pope or an ox? I have to put
on my cloak, carry the hat *and* sing! Don't any of you want
to sing? Have you come down with melancholia? Five
choirboys without voices? *(He turns to one of the imaginary
choirboys)* You, sing the lead part! *(He sings a few
notes, using the tonality of the first voice in the chorus:)*

Fet Serviciiiii . . .

(He does it again, conducting it with his head) First! *(Sings
as if he were the choirboy:)*

Fet Servici . . .

Hold the note!

Serviciiiiii . . .

(Turning to another imaginary choirboy) Second!

Un Rey Vindra Perpetual . . .

Hold the note . . .

Perpetuaaaaal . . .

(To another choirboy) Third!

Vestit de Nostra Carn Mortal . . .

Higher! *(To another choirboy)* Fourth!

Del Ziel Vindra Tot Certament.

(He performs a hallelujah chorus jumping from one tonality to another and, as the conductor of the chorus, transforms the song into a sequence of rebukes, scowls and threats. Then, pointing at the fifth chorister:)

Now do it again with the same tonality to back it up.

(And, as if he were the choirboy, he executes a kind of accompaniment on three notes that ends with the voice distorted in a high note sung off-key. He interrupts himself dismissively:)

Tone deaf!!! *(Alluding to the cloak)* Let's all push together. *(Sings in rising high notes:)*

Per Fer del Setgle Jugiament . . .

(He stops himself immediately) Tone deaf, shut up! You're completely off-key. You'll never become a priest because you can't sing the mass! You'll always stay a choirboy! Shut up and don't sing!

(Slicing the air with his outstretched hand he gives the order for absolute silence. To another choirboy:)

Fifth!

Per Fer del Setgle Jugiament . . .

Now everybody sing together and raise this cloak. Give me some support . . . You, tone deaf, don't sing!

(Still singing in the style of a Gregorian chant, he mimes the great effort it takes to lift the cloak onto his shoulders as he begins to walk:)

Al Jorn del Judici
Parra Qui Avra Fet Servici . . .

(He stops immediately and makes the gesture of yanking on the cloak. He is holding himself back, exhausted and furious.)

Who has their foot on my cloak? . . . *(He looks over his shoulder in a rage)* Tone deaf! Get off it! You can't sing! You're tone deaf! You don't lift up the cloak, and you put your feet on it . . . Watch out! . . . I've got my eye on you! . . . I'll nail you to the main door by your tongue! Tongue, nail, door, hammer—TON TON TON!

(He quickly mimes the action of the nailing, then proceeds to draw in the air an image of the choirboy nailed by his tongue swaying in the wind as he hangs. He lets out a groan that sounds like the door squeaking on its hinges:)

GGNAAA! AAAAA! GGNNAAAA! AAAAA! Watch out!
(Giving orders) Lift that cloak! *(Going back to the chant as he adjusts the cloak on his shoulders and ties the ribbons on his chest; exhausted)* What a tough job it is to be a pope! *(Continues singing:)*

Un Rey Vindra Perpetual . . .

(Giving orders) The cushion with the rings! *(Sings:)*

Vestit de Nostra Carn Mortal . . .

(He takes a ring, one of many, from the cushion that is given to him. He looks at the ring, and after putting it on

his finger, comments) Look how this one glistens! It gives off so many sparkles that you can't look at it. *(Goes back to the chant as he puts on rings from the index finger to the little finger. He exclaims)* It's too big . . . ah no . . . this one's for the thumb! *(Moves the ring from his little finger to his thumb)* Oh, that's better! *(Turning back to the imaginary choirboys)* Now prepare yourselves, so we can all begin on the same step! Sing!

(He goes back to his threatening gestures and his singing. He moves. Almost pushed, he finds himself thrust forward. With great effort he barely avoids ending up flat on his face on the floor. He gets up, re-adjusts his clothing, miter and cloak. Then he points ferociously at the dimwitted imaginary choirboy.)

Tone deaf! What are you doing pushing ahead when the others haven't started yet! Do you want to knock me onto the ground? Would you like to see the pope rolling around with his face in the mud . . . with his hat rammed down his throat so he can't breathe . . . Watch out!

(He repeats the pantomime of the nailing by the tongue, miniaturizing the gestures so that the choirboy is transformed into a puppet only a few centimeters tall. Resumes giving orders in a regal tone:)

Unfurl this cloak! Back up! Don't start right away . . . we sway a little first . . . pretend to begin, but don't begin! *(Mimes the movement he has described and begins)* Take a deep breath . . . move backwards . . . another breath, and then in the end one moves! I'm a pope, not a wagon! Watch out! *(Quickly acts out the pantomime of the nailing in a synthesized form)* Let's go! *(Goes back to the singing of the religious chant)* Begin . . . now backwards . . . *(He begins, taking a few majestic steps, still singing:)*

Un Rey Vindra Perpetual . . .

(He stops suddenly and looks around as if all the choirboys have run away) Oh, choirboys . . . where are you all going? You're leaving me in the middle of the street . . . all alone?! *(In another tone, to some choirboys who are coming back)* What is it? . . . Another procession?! . . . Another procession . . . Crossing mine?! Who's in the procession? Jesus? . ., Who is this Jesus? . . . ah, Christ! *(As if remembering, he suddenly slaps his hand against his forehead)* Jesus Christ! He has two names . . . keep them together so you don't confuse me! . . . *(As if watching Christ who is coming toward him with the cross on his shoulders)* Ah, he's the one under the cross . . . Dammit, look what they did to him! *(Sincerely saddened)* Look . . . all those thorns in his head . . . there's blood all over . . . they've spit on him . . . scratched him . . . beaten him . . . Now I know why they call him "poor Christ." *(Turning back to the choirboys, he lowers his head as if overwhelmed)* Brothers, carry me away from here, I can't look . . . it disturbs me too much to see these things . . . *(Pretending to respond to the advice of another prelate)* Eh? You think it's a good idea for me to go and meet him? . . . Why? . . . Oh, for the people! That's right, so the people will see us together and say, "Oh, they know each other . . . they go to the same church!" You're right. *(Taking off his hat, cloak and rings)* Take them. Take the hat, take the cloak . . . Take the rings . . . He's crazy, that man! He can't stand priests wearing things that shine! *(Bends over in a gesture of grabbing a handful of mud)* Give me, give me some dirt . . . *(Responding angrily)* To dirty myself up! *(He smears mud on his face and clothes, and then points to Jesus)* He's a madman, a sophist full of horrible fixations! He only likes people who are miserable, downtrodden and filthy whores . . . *(Moving away from the choirboys)* Leave me. Go over there . . . way over there! I have no need for accompaniment . . . I'm going alone! . . . *(Approaches Christ with a big mischievous smile)* How are you doing, Jesus? . . . Eh? Who am I? *(To the choirboys)* Oh, he doesn't recognize me! *(To Christ)* I'm the pope . . . Boniface Maximus . . . Prince of the Church of Rome . . . po-ope!

(To the choirboys) He's forgotten what a pope is! He's a little shaken up! *(To Christ)* Pope! Po-ope! *(In a conciliatory tone)* Don't you remember what you said to Peter: "Peter, now that we have a Church, let's make someone the leader of the Church. And you, you will be the first leader . . . who we will call the pope . . . After you die, there will be another pope, then" *(Rhythmically)* "a pope, a death, a pope, a death, a pope . . ." *(Pause)* "a potpourri! . . ." *(As if listening to the comments of Jesus, he assumes an attitude of astonishment, barely able to hold back a laugh)* You never said that to Peter? So, he must have made that up! *(His laughter explodes riotously. He suddenly stops himself, acting surprised, listening to what Christ is saying)* Eh?! Me?! I murdered monks? That's not true! Who told you that? *(Angry and threatening)* Give me the name of the man who told you that, and I'll wring his neck and smash his skull . . . *(Makes gesture of catching the spy, twisting his neck and drilling a finger into his head. He stops and mimes an attempt to disown the violent gesture by plugging up the hole in the head of his victim)* No, Jesus, I love monks. Every morning when I wake up— *(Turns to a choirboy)* Go get me a monk . . . *(Turning back to Christ)* I kiss a monk . . . every morning! *(Giving orders to the choirboy)* Go get me that monk! . . . *(Listens to the reply of the choirboy; impatiently)* Then un-nail his tongue from the main door! *(He stops himself, realizing the horror of his mistake. Then he changes his tone, gets down on his knees in front of Christ and speaks with desperate humility)* Jesus, you're right . . . I am the worst man in the world . . . a scoundrel . . . a thief . . . a good-for-nothing . . . but you who are so good and kind enough to have granted forgiveness to all the wretches, murderers and whores of the earth . . . can you give forgiveness also to me, your son . . . do it so that all the people can see . . . you and me, under the same cross . . . me helping you to carry it. *(Squeezes his way under the cross, trying to lift it)* Get your ass out of here, Cirenius! I'm strong . . . I carry those heavy cloaks! *(Tries to resist Christ who is evidently pushing him out from underneath the cross)* Don't chase me awaaaaaaaaay!

(Receiving a tremendous kick in the butt, he finds himself literally propelled to the other side of the stage) Christ! Kicking me?! The pope?! Have you gone mad?! *(Turns to the heavens)* If your father knew, poor man! . . . *(Points his finger at the audience)* Ah, you enjoy seeing all these people laugh behind my back. *(Full of spite)* The day will come when you will be nailed to the cross . . . On that day I will be so tremendously delighted that I will go whoring, and get myself shit-faced drunk! *(Pointing his finger at Christ)* King of the Asses! I am the Prince! The Crowned Prince of the Church of Rome! *(Gives orders to the choirboys)* Give me the big hat . . . pass me the cloak . . . hand me the rings . . . *(To Christ)* Look how they sparkle! I am the Prince! And you are the King of the Asses! *(In a stentorian voice)* Hail, hail praise to the Crowned Prince Boniface . . . Glory! Glory to Boniface! Sing!

(He leaves triumphantly with his chest out, singing the Gregorian chant at the top of his voice:)

Laude Bonifax Maximo
Prenze Romana Eglesia
Magnificat et Exultet.

(All hail Boniface the Great
Prince of the Church of Rome
Magnificent and exalted.)

(The lights dim slowly.)

RON JENKINS has investigated comic traditions in Italy, Indonesia, Lithuania, Israel, South Africa and Japan with the support of fellowships from the Watson Foundation, the Danforth Foundation, Harvard University's Sheldon Fund and the Asian Cultural Council of the Rockefeller Brothers Foundation. He holds a doctorate from Harvard and a masters in buffoonery from the Ringling Brothers Clown College. His translations of plays by Dario Fo and Joshua Sobol have been staged at American Repertory Theatre, Yale Repertory Theatre, New York Theatre Workshop and the Royal Shakespeare Company. He is the author of *Acrobats of the Soul* and *Subversive Laughter*, as well as numerous articles on comedy and culture for the *Drama Review*, *Kyoto Review*, *American Theatre*, *Village Voice*, *New York Times* and other publications. A former circus clown and juggler, Jenkins is currently professor of theatre at Wesleyan University in Connecticut. His book *Dario Fo and Franca Rame: Artful Laughter* (Aperture, New York) was published in 2001 with the support of a fellowship from the John Simon Guggenheim Memorial Foundation.